PRINT'S BEST POSTERS & BILLBOARDS

Library of Congress
Catalog Card Number 94-067195
ISBN 0-915734-96-6

RC PUBLICATIONS

President and Publisher: Howard Cadel
Vice President and Editor: Martin Fox
Creative Director: Andrew Kner
Managing Director, Book Projects: Linda Silver
Administrative Assistant: Nancy Silver
Assistant Art Director: Michele L. Trombley

Print's Best
POSTERS &
BILLBOARDS

WINNING DESIGNS FROM PRINT MAGAZINE'S NATIONAL COMPETITION

Edited by
LINDA SILVER

Introduction by
JOYCE RUTTER KAYE

Designed by
ANDREW KNER

Published by
RC PUBLICATIONS, INC.
NEW YORK, NY

Posters, broadsides, billboards, 30-sheets…Outdoor, or "out of home," advertising comes in many sizes and guises, from hastily-scrawled "man with van" handbills tacked on lampposts to lushly illustrated posters for regional theater groups. But regardless of what it's called, all outdoor advertising shares one simple objective: to communicate a message instantly and with impact, to a mass audience.

To advertisers, the lure of outdoor is growing stronger these days since that mass audience is getting more fragmented and difficult to reach through traditional channels, like network television. With the onslaught of cable television, interactive advertising, and so-called "narrowcasting," the great outdoors appears to be the last frontier to reach the masses. In many ways, outdoor has come full circle: In the 1920s, when marketing products across the country first became widespread, posters were the most pervasive form of advertising.

Today, growing numbers of retail, automotive, service and entertainment industries and packaged goods marketers are venturing into the field to join the cigarette advertisers who have long dominated the category. (Now, Joe Camel can wink at Marky Mark grabbing at his Calvin Klein-ed crotch in Times Square.) Retailers in particular are flocking to outdoor media. According to Advertising Age, during the first half of 1993, retail ad spending in outdoor markets was up 154 per cent from the same period a year before. Overall, outdoor ad spending was up 2.2 per cent.

With this renewed interest in taking ads outdoors, it would seem to follow that all that fresh air would breathe some creative life into those offerings. Indeed, many advertisers are not only taking advantage of using outdoor, they are also looking for innovative ways to manipulate its standard rectangular format. Several years ago, for example, Wieden & Kennedy played up the name of Michael Jordan's Air Jordan sneaker line—and his gravity-defying athleticism—by showing him slamming a basketball high above the traditional confines of the standard 12'-by-24' billboard. In New York City, the Bronx Zoo recently utilized the triangle dome on taxis by showing an image of a giraffe who appeared to burst through the roof. In a similar vein, McCall's magazine created an optical illusion by plastering an ad on the passenger door of a cab showing the torso of a woman who was seated in a car, reading an issue of the magazine.

Advertisers have also used the format to play before/after teaser games with viewers. In the early 1990s, NYNEX Yellow Pages ads from Chiat/Day plastered copy-free images all over New York City, followed up by the same images

4

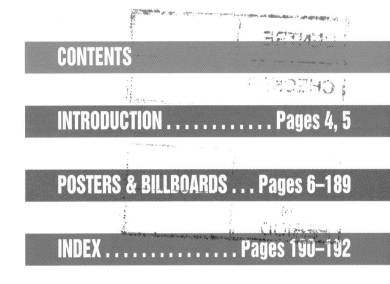

with word plays on the directory's advertisers. An image of a blue bunny, for example, was later revealed to be an ad for a "hair dye." For KISW Rock Radio in Seattle, Cooper/Lusk Studios created a teaser campaign with one billboard covered completely with the words "Blah, blah, blah, blah…" A follow-up showed an electric guitar literally bursting through the babble with the headline: "More Pure Rock! No Useless Talk."

Transit media in urban areas is also a good place to witness experimentation. True, the subway cars have a fair share of hilariously repulsive two-color sideboards blaring "Torn Earlobe?" or "Hemorrhoids? Call MD-Tusch" assaulting legions of bleary-eyed straphangers. But riders can also find glimmers of inspiration and entertainment underground. For years, New York City's Transit Authority has sponsored a "Transit in Motion" series appearing in subways and buses that feature poems from a vast selection of known and unknown writers. The same department has also sponsored a wildly popular bilingual comic strip series called "La Decision/The Decision" about two young lovers struggling with the issue of AIDS in their relationship.

On the high end, posters created by graphic designers and illustrators for arts organizations, theater groups, and charitable causes often serve as an optimal showcase for the artist, as they have since the early days of this century. James Victore's black-and-white *Romeo and Juliet* poster for the Shakespeare Project theater company, for example, is an exercise in simplicity with its illustration of a single rose on a black background. And actors in the Joseph Papp Public Theatre have been said to negotiate an appearance in one of Paul Davis's powerful posters as part of their contract .

Of course, the most obvious sign that outdoor has come to the fore is the fact the medium is parodying itself. A recent poster for Texas Textbooks from the Austin agency GSD&M shows a brick wall with a handbill advertising "Answers to every test on campus" and a phone number to tear off. And the downtown Manhattan agency Mad Dogs & Englishmen took the joke one step further with its ad for the Tiny Mythic Theatre Company. The canary yellow poster is designed to look like a summons handed to those who illegally plaster handbills on public property, reading, "This Poster is in Violation of NYC Dept. of Sanitation Code #1-8075." In its sheer brashness, this deliberate eyesore seems to underscore one important aspect of this particular medium: that subtlety is best left in the back pages of The New Yorker. Outdoors, you need to shout.—*Joyce Rutter Kaye*

AGENCY:

The Traver Company,

Seattle, Washington

ART DIRECTOR:

Anne Traver

DESIGNERS:

Kristine Matthews,

Anne Traver

ILLUSTRATOR:

Gregory Grenon

HAND LETTERING:

Kristine Matthews

PRODUCTION MANAGER:

Evan Konecky

PRINTER: Ink on Paper

PURPOSE: To promote an

art exhibit.

GREGORY GRENON
WILLIAM TRAVER GALLERY
OCTOBER '93   110 UNION

William Traver Gallery

FACE2FACE

AGENCY:

Bob Wright Creative Group,

Rochester, New York

ART DIRECTOR:

Bob Whiting

DESIGNERS: Bob Whiting,

Jim Mattiucci, Bryan

Charles (invitation)

ILLUSTRATOR/

PHOTOGRAPHER:

Jim Mattiucci

PRINTING PROCESS:

4-color

PURPOSE: To promote

Bob Wright Creative

Group and Bob Wright

Productions (multi-image

division) joint open house

for clients. The graphics

were part of an effort to

attach a personality to the

name by utilizing photo-

illustrated portraits of

employees, along with

short bios and

straightforward black-

and-white portraits.

The Bob Wright Creative Group

Cover (far left) and spread (left) from desk calendar that was part of the promotional campaign.

DESIGN FIRM:

Vaughn/Wedeen Creative,

Albuquerque, New Mexico

ART DIRECTOR:

Steve Wedeen

DESIGNER/ILLUSTRATOR:

Lisa Graff

QUANTITY: 100

PRINTING PROCESS:

Silkscreen

PURPOSE: To promote

and present the fall

campaign to the

company's sales team.

Cover of campaign sales guide.

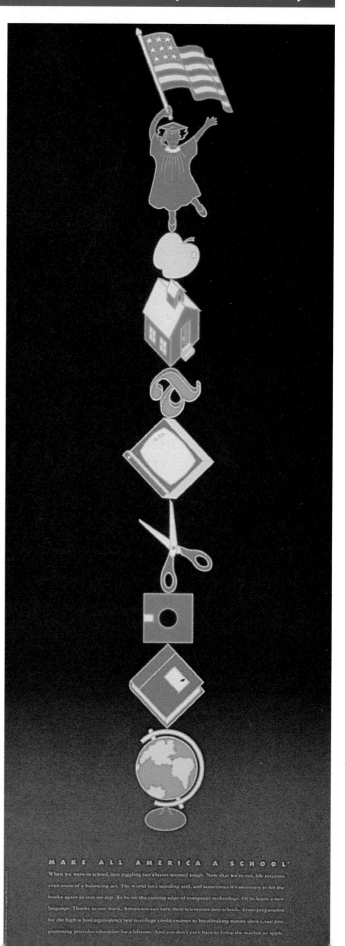

Annual festival sponsored by the Hispanic Heritage Foundation.

DESIGN FIRM:
Robert Guthrie Illustration, New Orleans, Louisiana

ART DIRECTOR/
DESIGNER/ILLUSTRATOR:
Robert Guthrie

QUANTITY: 500

PRINTING PROCESS:
Serigraph

PURPOSE:
Commemorative poster for sale at the event.

SUMMER'S COOL

Continuing Education • University of Utah

DESIGN FIRM:

DCE Graphic Design,

Salt Lake City, Utah

ART DIRECTOR:

Scott Greer

DESIGNER/ILLUSTRATOR:

Lisa A. Brashear

COPYWRITER: Joan Levy

BUDGET: $10,667.25

QUANTITY: 28 billboards

PRINTING PROCESS:

Silkscreen on 30-sheet

billboard format

PURPOSE: To encourage

students to take summer

classes.

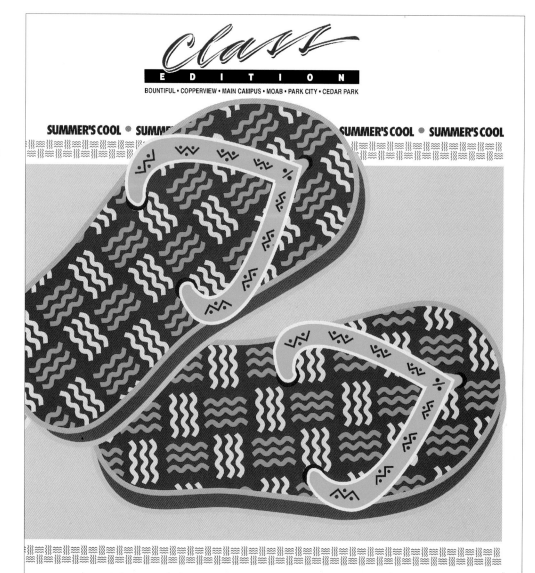

Tiny record store on New York's Lower East Side specializing in alternative bands.

AGENCY:

Capitalist Conspiracy Advertising,

Long Island City, New York

ART DIRECTOR/

DESIGNER/

PHOTOGRAPHER/

COPYWRITER: Greg Cerny

QUANTITY:

2 of each poster

PRINTING PROCESS:

IRIS prints

PURPOSE: To attract the attention of people passing by the store and let them know the type of music they could find inside.

Reconstruction Records

The Women by Clare Boothe Luce   Directed by Anne Bogart   January 1 - February 5, 1994   Charge by Phone: 527 - 5151   50 Church Street, Hartford, Connecticut

THE WOMEN

HartfordStage.

AGENCY:

Keiler Design Group,

Farmington, Connecticut

ART DIRECTOR/

DESIGNER:

Christopher Passehl

PHOTOGRAPHER:

Jim Coon

MODEL: Laila Robins

MAKE-UP: Linda McGovern

QUANTITY: 500

PRINTING PROCESS:

Offset lithography; two

blacks (duotone) and

PMS red

PURPOSE: To promote

awareness of an all-female

play through the use of a

black-and-white fashion

image evoking the 1930s,

the era in which the play

was written.

Hartford Stage

Arte de Huichol

- Exhibition and sale of Huichol Indian ceremonial and folk art

  Proceeds will benefit Mexico's Huichol Family Agricultural Program

- November 14-15, 1992
  10am to 6pm
  100 Hamilton Avenue
  (corner of Alma)
  Palo Alto

Charitable organization working with the Huichol Indians in Mexico.

DESIGN FIRM:
Lauren Smith Design,
Palo Alto, California

DESIGNER: Lauren Smith

PHOTOGRAPHER:
Mel Lindstrom

PRINTER:
Guardian Printing

BUDGET: Pro bono

QUANTITY:
Approximately 1000

PRINTING PROCESS:
Offset

PURPOSE: To promote a
Huichol art show fundraiser.

Amistad Foundation

Vertical Butt Stroke to groin.

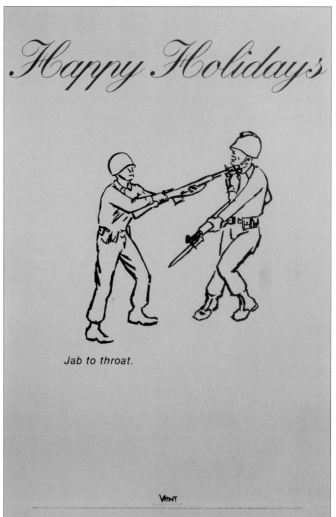

Jab to throat.

Smash to face.

14

Seasons Greetings

Smash to face.

A non-profit group dedicated to pointing out political and moral inconsistencies in society.
DESIGN FIRM: After Hours, Phoenix, Arizona
ART DIRECTORS: Russ Haan, Todd Fedell
DESIGNER: Todd Fedell
ILLUSTRATION: U.S. Marine Corps
BUDGET: $1000
QUANTITY: 100 of each poster
PRINTING PROCESS: Silkscreen
PURPOSE: Holiday greeting promotion.

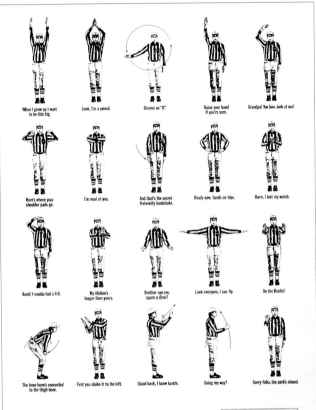

AGENCY:

Clarity Coverdale Fury

Advertising, Inc.,

Minneapolis, Minnesota

ART DIRECTOR/

ILLUSTRATOR:

Randy Hughes

COPYWRITER:

Josh Denberg

AGENCY: Martin/Williams,
Minneapolis, Minnesota

ART DIRECTOR:
Jim Henderson

COPYWRITER:
Chris Preston

PURPOSE: To announce
an across-the-board
price-cut of all merchandise.

AGENCY:
McCann-Erickson/
Seattle, Washington

CREATIVE DIRECTOR:
Jim Walker

ART DIRECTOR:
Kevin Nolan

PHOTOGRAPHER:
Don Mason

COPYWRITER:
Brett Borders

PURPOSE: Promotional

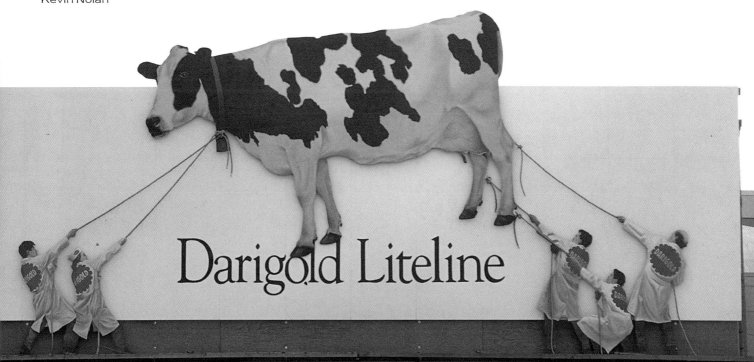

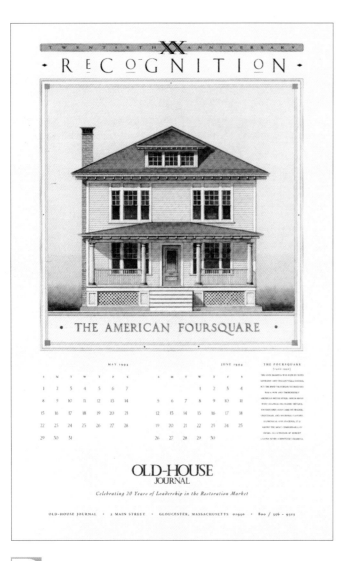

RECOGNITION
THE AMERICAN FOURSQUARE

OLD-HOUSE
JOURNAL

Celebrating 20 Years of Leadership in the Restoration Market

OLD-HOUSE JOURNAL · 2 MAIN STREET · GLOUCESTER, MASSACHUSETTS 01930 · 800 / 356 - 9313

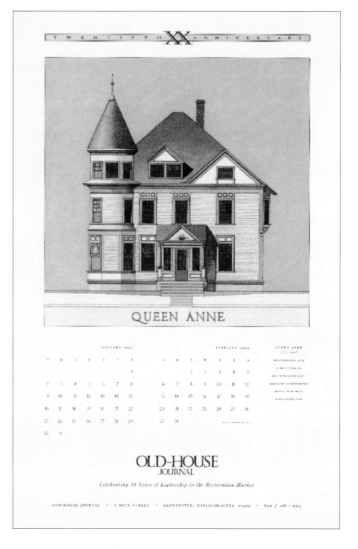

QUEEN ANNE

OLD-HOUSE
JOURNAL

Celebrating 20 Years of Leadership in the Restoration Market

OLD-HOUSE JOURNAL · 2 MAIN STREET · GLOUCESTER, MASSACHUSETTS 01930 · 800 / 356 - 9313

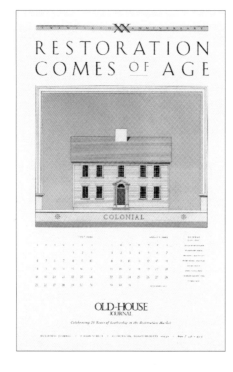

RESTORATION COMES OF AGE
COLONIAL

OLD-HOUSE
JOURNAL

Celebrating 20 Years of Leadership in the Restoration Market

OLD-HOUSE JOURNAL · 2 MAIN STREET · GLOUCESTER, MASSACHUSETTS 01930 · 800 / 356 - 9313

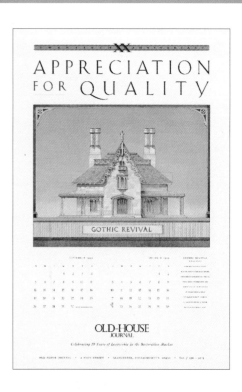

APPRECIATION FOR QUALITY
GOTHIC REVIVAL

OLD-HOUSE
JOURNAL

Celebrating 20 Years of Leadership in the Restoration Market

OLD-HOUSE JOURNAL · 2 MAIN STREET · GLOUCESTER, MASSACHUSETTS 01930 · 800 / 356 - 9313

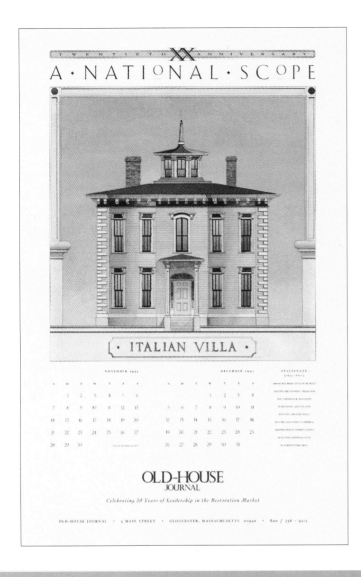

DESIGN FIRM:

Dovetale Publishers,

Gloucester, Massachusetts

ART DIRECTOR:

Patrick Mitchell

DESIGNER:

Inga Soderberg

ILLUSTRATOR:

Robert Leanna

PURPOSE: Twentieth

anniversary promotion.

AGENCY:

Mithoff Advertising, Inc.,

El Paso, Texas

ART DIRECTOR/

DESIGNER/ILLUSTRATOR:

Clive Cochran

PRINTER:

IMS Industries, Inc.

TYPE OUTPUT:

RJ Typesetters

BUDGET: Pro bono

QUANTITY: 250

PRINTING PROCESS:

Silkscreen

PURPOSE: Art faculty

exhibit announcement.

DESIGN FIRM: After Hours,

Phoenix, Arizona

ART DIRECTOR:

Russ Haan

DESIGNER/ILLUSTRATOR:

Brad Smith

BUDGET: $3000

QUANTITY: 300

PRINTING PROCESS:

Silkscreen

PURPOSE: Call-for-entries

for an annual creative

writing competition.

Regular   Unleaded

1993 CREATIVE WRITING COMPETITION CALL FOR ENTRIES

For more information and entry forms contact your English Department, Dean of Students or Student Services Office.

Sponsored by The Maricopa Community Colleges. The Maricopa Community Colleges abide by all state and federal non-discrimination and equal opportunity requirements.

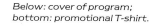

DESIGNER/ILLUSTRATOR:

Vicki Rollo, Sarasota, Florida

ART DIRECTOR:

Deena Frankel

PRINTING PROCESS:

Offset lithography

PURPOSE: Promotional; design was used for posters, T-shirts, buttons, and ads in Variety and French publications.

JUILLIARD

Photograph Henry Wolf

Below: cover of Pre-College Division brochure and application.

DESIGN FIRM:

Jessica Weber Design, Inc.,

New York, New York

ART DIRECTOR:

Jessica Weber

DESIGNER: Orlando Adiao

PHOTOGRAPHER:

Henry Wolf

QUANTITY: 2500

PRINTING PROCESS:

Offset

PURPOSE: Promotional

The Juilliard School

DESIGN FIRM:

Peter Good Graphic Design,

Chester, Connecticut

ART DIRECTOR/

DESIGNER/ILLUSTRATOR:

Peter Good

PHOTOGRAPHER:

Jim Coon

PURPOSE: Promotional

poster for series of TV

programs about

Connecticut.

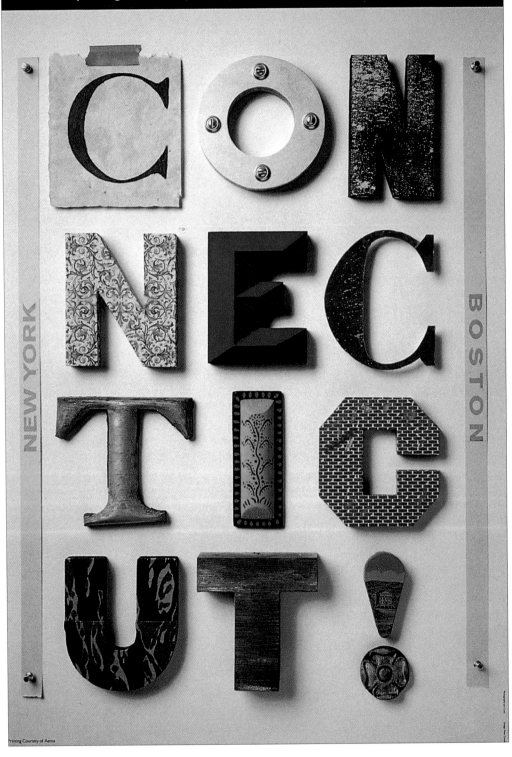

Connecticut Public Television

DESIGN FIRM:

Peter Good Graphic Design,

Chester, Connecticut

ART DIRECTOR/

DESIGNER: Peter Good

PURPOSE: Promotional

poster for '93-'94 season.

TheaterWorks

DESIGN FIRM:

Peter Good Graphic Design,

Chester, Connecticut

ART DIRECTOR/

DESIGNER/ILLUSTRATOR:

Peter Good

PURPOSE: Promotional

poster for '92-'93 season.

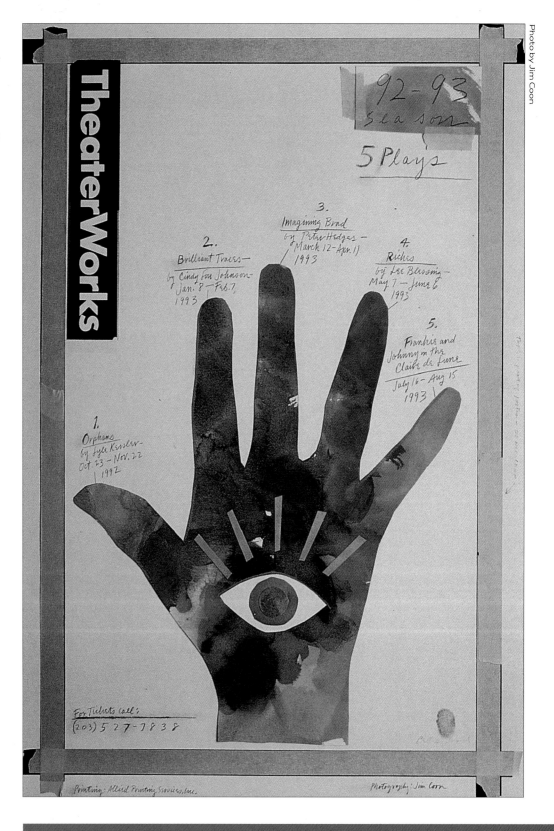

DESIGN FIRM:

Peter Good Graphic Design,

Chester, Connecticut

ART DIRECTOR/

DESIGNER: Peter Good

PURPOSE: Promotional

poster for production of

Scotland Road.

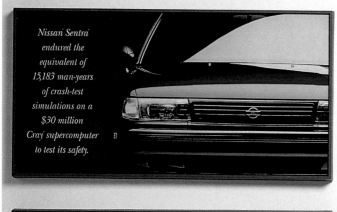

Nissan Sentra endured the equivalent of 15,183 man-years of crash-test simulations on a $30 million Cray supercomputer to test its safety.

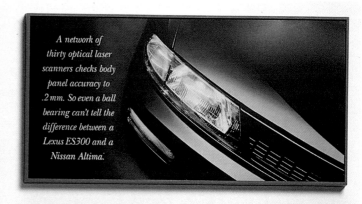

A network of thirty optical laser scanners checks body panel accuracy to .2 mm. So even a ball bearing can't tell the difference between a Lexus ES300 and a Nissan Altima.

The Nissan 240SX doesn't look like Japan Rail's bullet train. But their aerodynamics were both crafted in the world's fastest wind tunnel – ours.

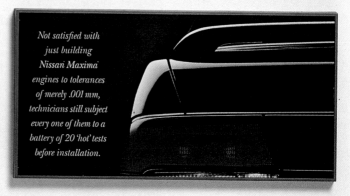

Not satisfied with just building Nissan Maxima engines to tolerances of merely .001 mm, technicians still subject every one of them to a battery of 20 'hot' tests before installation.

Nissan Motor Corporation in USA (Automotive)

DESIGN FIRM:

The Designory, Inc.,

Long Beach, California

ART DIRECTOR/

DESIGNER: Gary Valenti

PURPOSE: Point-of-sale

posters for 1994 Nissan.

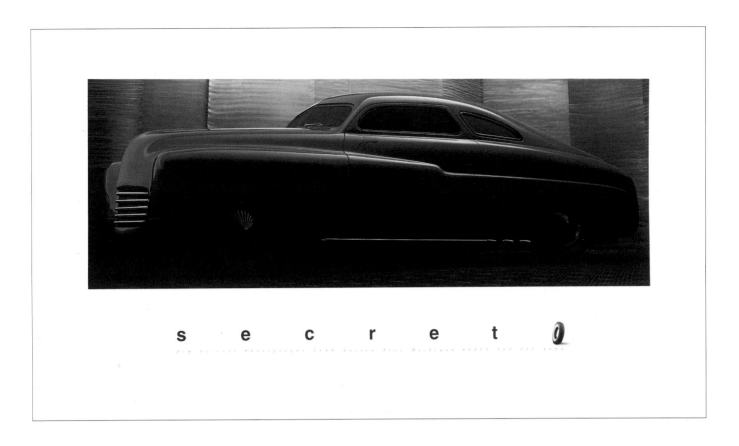

s e c r e t o

Jim Secreto Photography (Automotive Photography)

PHOTOGRAPHER:

Jim Secreto,

Troy, Michigan

ART DIRECTOR:

Coomes Dudek

DESIGNER: John Dudek

PURPOSE: Self-promotion

Self-promotion mailer.

DESIGN FIRM:

Visual Arts Press Ltd.,

New York, New York

ART DIRECTOR:

Silas Rhodes

DESIGNER: Paul Davis

QUANTITY: 2650

PURPOSE: Promotional

THE END FEST
THE BEASTIE BOYS

So you get up every CHARLATANS U.K.
morning and your head hurts SONIC YOUTH
and your muscles ache TOAD THE WET SPROCKET
and your breath smells really
bad and you wonder what's
the point is there a god here
and you gotta go to work and you're
late and it's raining and you brush your teeth
but you get the feeling that the rotten stuff inside you is still
there and you wonder what's the point where is all this headed and on the way
to work you see this poster that tells you about all the cool
bands playing in one place on one day
and for a moment a shimmering
ray of light comes through the
clouds and you think wow every day contained
the prospect of being this momentous, this grand,
this focused then maybe getting up in the morning might not seem
like such a huge drag and you continue on to work

MUDHONEY and you think
hey that was
L7
pretty long poster and
THE POSIES now really late. Shit. Screw that damn poster.
SATURDAY AUGUST 8, 1992 KITSAP
SARAH McLACHLAN COUNTY FAIRGROUNDS BREMERTON WA

THE END 107.7

Budweiser

AGENCY: Cole & Weber,
Seattle, Washington
ART DIRECTOR:
Steve Luker
ILLUSTRATOR:
Gary Baseman
COPYWRITER:
Kevin Jones
PRODUCTION MANAGER:
Wanda Nichols
BUDGET: $5000
QUANTITY: 3000
PRINTING PROCESS:
Offset
PURPOSE: To publicize
the station's day-long
concert event.

DESIGN FIRM:

Stewart Monderer

Design, Inc.,

Boston, Massachusetts

ART DIRECTOR/

DESIGNER:

Stewart Monderer

ILLUSTRATOR:

Seymour Chwast

PRINTER:

United Lithograph

PAPER: Champion Benefit,

natural flax

QUANTITY: 2500

PRINTING PROCESS:

Sheet-fed offset

PURPOSE: Poster/mailer

promoting AIGA/Boston

"Issues and Causes"

exhibition which featured

work that underscored the

importance of effective

graphic design in

communicating a message.

AGENCY: Evans Group, Salt Lake City, Utah

ART DIRECTORS: Dick Brown, Steve Cardon (Date's a Dog)

DESIGNER: Dick Brown

ILLUSTRATORS: Dick Brown (If You See Gus), Dale Kilbourn (Van Go)

PHOTOGRAPHERS: Roger Tuttle (Prizm), Ed Rosenberger (Date's a Dog, Zipper)

COPYWRITERS: Dick Brown, Steve Cardon (Date's a Dog)

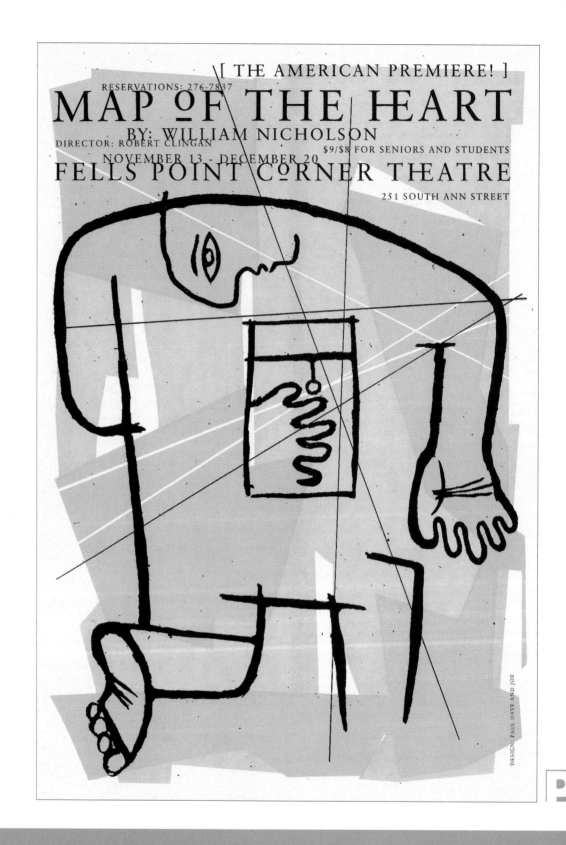

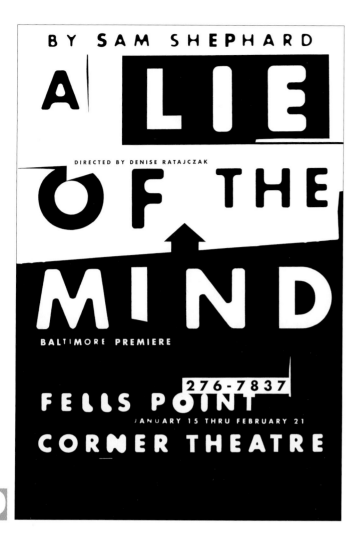

DESIGN FIRM:

David Plunkert Studio,

Baltimore, Maryland

DESIGNERS: Joe Parisi

(Map of the Heart), Paul

Sahre, Dave Plunkert

BUDGET: Pro bono

QUANTITY: 200

PRINTING PROCESS:

Screen print

PURPOSE: To promote

local theater productions.

Fells Point Corner Theatre

AGENCY:

The Martin Agency,

Richmond, Virginia

ART DIRECTOR:

Mark Fuller

PHOTOGRAPHER:

Craig Anderson

COPYWRITER:

Tripp Westbrook

PRINT PRODUCER:

Melissa Ralston

"For some reason I've never had much of a problem with shoplifters."

AAA Pawn (Pawnbroker)

BUDGET:

$2200 (for printing)

QUANTITY: 250

PRINTING PROCESS:

Duotone with black and

PMS 301, plus PMS 185

and spot gloss varnish

lithography

PURPOSE: Promotional—

local pawn shop wanted to

increase public awareness

of its business.

"My shop is like a bank. It's got a lobby, a safe, and an S.O.B. in the loan department."

"My 'Satisfaction Guaranteed' policy: You buy it. I'm satisfied."

36

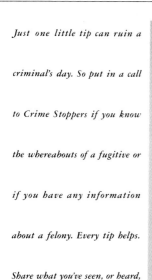

Just one little tip can ruin a criminal's day. So put in a call to Crime Stoppers if you know the whereabouts of a fugitive or if you have any information about a felony. Every tip helps. Share what you've seen, or heard, or found. Give us a license plate number, a name or a physical

description. Anything that can help us put Austin's criminals behind bars. If your tip leads to a felony arrest and a grand jury indictment, we'll pay you up to

$1,000. For your protection, we won't ask your name. And you won't have to testify in court.

AND YOU THOUGHT WAITRESSES COMPLAINED ABOUT TIPS.

If you wish to make a tax-deductible donation to Crime Stoppers, call us at 474-4709.

Photograph is not of an actual criminal.

Austin Crime Stoppers (Community Watch Group)

AGENCY:

GSD&M Advertising,

Austin, Texas

ART DIRECTOR:

David Crawford

PHOTOGRAPHER:

David Mayfield

COPYWRITER:

Brian Brooker

BUDGET: $2000

QUANTITY: 1000 of five

different posters

PRINTING PROCESS:

Black and gray duotone

PURPOSE: To promote

public awareness.

The colors are okay. But we'd prefer the image of a toxic dump.

BOY IS THAT AN UGLY SHIRT.™

Some colors take your breath away. We're looking for people to lose their lunch.

BOY IS THAT AN UGLY SHIRT.™

In nature you can find beauty, balance, and subtle color. Frankly, we don't get it.

BOY IS THAT AN UGLY SHIRT.™

Boy is that an Ugly Shirt (Clothing)

AGENCY:

Hoffman York & Compton,

Milwaukee, Wisconsin

ART DIRECTOR/

DESIGNER: Barb Paulini

COPYWRITER:

Tom Jordan

PHOTOGRAPHERS:

Mitsuo Kazama, Dick

Baker, Koju Yamashita

DESIGN FIRM:

Bailey Lauerman &

Associates,

Lincoln, Nebraska

ART DIRECTOR/

DESIGNER: Carter Weitz

PHOTOGRAPHER:

Don Farrall

COPYWRITER:

Mitch Koch

ILLUSTRATOR:

Joe McDermott

BUDGET: Pro bono

QUANTITY: 800

PRINTING PROCESS:

4-color offset

PURPOSE: Give-away to

marathon participants.

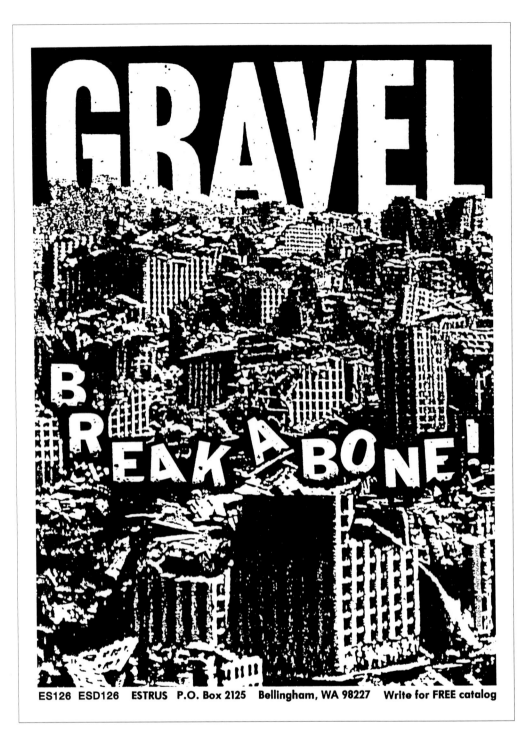

GRAVEL

B REAK A BONE!

ES126 ESD126 ESTRUS P.O. Box 2125 Bellingham, WA 98227 Write for FREE catalog

DESIGNER: Art Chantry,

Seattle, Washington

BUDGET: $50

QUANTITY: 1000

PRINTING PROCESS: Cheap

PURPOSE: To promote

the group's new record

Break-a-Bone

David Crider/Estrus Records (Record Label)

Coca-Cola USA

AGENCY:

GSD&M Advertising,

Austin, Texas

ART DIRECTOR:

Doug Lyon

PHOTOGRAPHER:

Rusty Hill

ILLUSTRATORS:

Doug Lyon, Elliott Park

COPYWRITER:

David Crawford

BUDGET: $250,000

QUANTITY: As needed

PRINTING PROCESS:

4-color

PURPOSE:

New campaign/position

for Mr. Pibb.

Dallas Society of Visual Communications

DESIGN FIRM:

Sullivan Perkins,

Dallas, Texas

ART DIRECTOR/

ILLUSTRATOR: Art Garcia

COPYWRITER:

Mark Perkins

QUANTITY: 700

PRINTING PROCESS:

4 flat colors

PURPOSE: To promote a

speaking engagement by

Art Chantry.

41

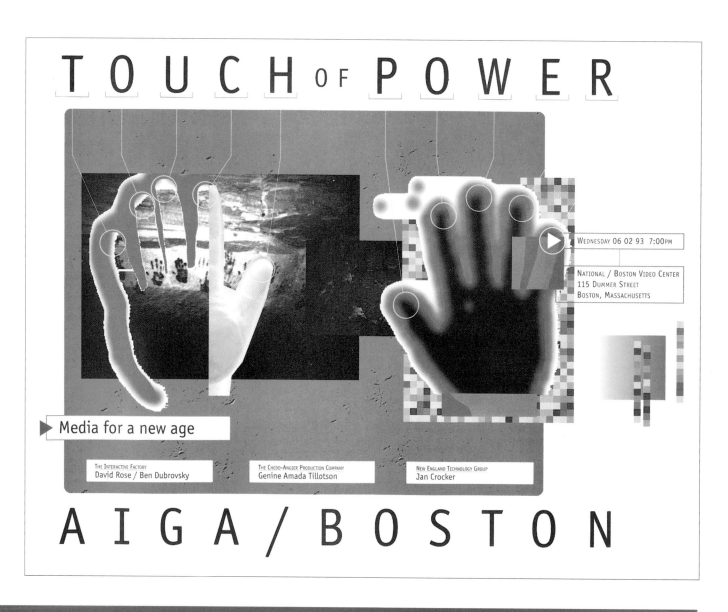

TOUCH OF POWER

WEDNESDAY 06 02 93 7:00PM

NATIONAL / BOSTON VIDEO CENTER
115 DUMMER STREET
BOSTON, MASSACHUSETTS

▶ Media for a new age

THE INTERACTIVE FACTORY
David Rose / Ben Dubrovsky

THE CHEDD-ANGIER PRODUCTION COMPANY
Genine Amada Tillotson

NEW ENGLAND TECHNOLOGY GROUP
Jan Crocker

AIGA/BOSTON

AIGA/Boston

DESIGN FIRM:

Marc English:Design,

Lexington, Massachusetts

DESIGNER/

PHOTOGRAPHER:

Marc English

PREPRESS:

Graphics Express

PRINTER: Williams Printing

BUDGET: Pro bono

QUANTITY: 2000

PRINTING PROCESS:

4-color offset

PURPOSE: To inform the

community about a multi-

media event.

DESIGN FIRM:

David Plunkert Studio,

Baltimore, Maryland

DESIGNER/

PHOTOGRAPHER:

Dave Plunkert

PRINTER:

Strine Printing

BUDGET: Pro bono

QUANTITY: 3000

PRINTING PROCESS:

Offset lithography

PURPOSE: To advertise a

panel discussion between

four prominent designers.

AIGA/Baltimore

Blue Cross & Blue Shield of Rhode Island

AGENCY:

Pagano Schenck & Kay,

Boston, Massachusetts

CREATIVE DIRECTOR:

Woody Kay

ART DIRECTOR:

Robert Hamilton, Woody

Kay (Unsightly Bulge)

COPYWRITER:

Bob Shiffrar

DESIGN FIRM:

The Martin Agency,

Richmond, Virginia

ART DIRECTOR:

Mark Fuller

COPYWRITER:

Kerry Feuerman

PHOTOGRAPHER:

David Langley

PRINT PRODUCER:

Linda Locks

ACCOUNT EXECUTIVE:

Todd Foutz

QUANTITY: 1100

PRINTING PROCESS:

Offset

PURPOSE: To remind
Mercedes owners that
precisely built cars like
theirs deserves only top-
quality, genuine Mercedes
parts.

AGENCY:

GSD&M Advertising,

Austin, Texas

ART DIRECTOR:

David Crawford

COPYWRITER:

Oscar Casares

BUDGET: $300

QUANTITY: 500

PRINTING PROCESS:

4-color

PURPOSE: Internal

promotion; also used as

magazine ad.

Dear Texas Monthly:

As a child, one of my earliest memories is seeing all of my big haired aunts in a buffet line.

(ONE READER'S RESPONSE TO OUR STORY ON THE TEXAS PHENOMENON KNOWN AS BIG HAIR, "HOORAY FOR BIG HAIR!," DECEMBER 1992.)

WE TALK ABOUT TEXAS. TEXAS TALKS ABOUT US.

Texas Monthly

DESIGN FIRM:

Ben & Jerry's

Creative Department,

Waterbury , Vermont

ART DIRECTOR:

Lyn Severance

DESIGNER/ILLUSTRATOR:

Cathie Dinsmore

BUDGET: $2500

QUANTITY: 200

PURPOSE: To advertise

annual Mother's Day event.

Ben & Jerry's (Ice Cream/Frozen Yogurt)

ART DIRECTOR/

DESIGNER:

Guido Brouwers/Nike,

Beaverton, Oregon

ILLUSTRATOR:

Philip Burke

PURPOSE: Promotional

AGENCY:

Russek Advertising,

New York, New York

ART DIRECTOR:

Jim Russek

DESIGNER/ILLUSTRATOR:

James McMullan

PURPOSE: To promote a

theater production

DESIGN FIRM:

Muller & Company,

Kansas City, Missouri

ART DIRECTOR:

John Muller

DESIGNERS: David Shultz,

David Marks

PHOTOGRAPHER:

Hollis Officer

BUDGET: Pro bono

QUANTITY: 3000

PRINTING PROCESS:

Lithography

PURPOSE: To publicize an

urban design competition.

Municipal Art Commission/Kansas City

THINK OF IT AS A DO NOT DISTURB SIGN.

BERNIE'S TATTOOING

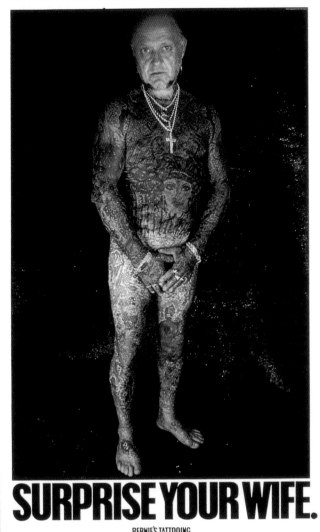

SURPRISE YOUR WIFE.

BERNIE'S TATTOOING

Bernie's Tattooing (Tattoo Parlor)

THE '90s VERSION OF BURNING YOUR BRA.

BERNIE'S TATTOOING

AGENCY:

The Martin Agency,

Richmond, Virginia

ART DIRECTOR: Jelly Helm

PHOTOGRAPHER:

Rick Dubin

COPYWRITER:

Raymond McKinney

PRINT PRODUCER:

Jenny Schoenherr

BUDGET: $3700

QUANTITY: 500

PRINTING PROCESS:

Sheet-fed, 4-color plus

aqueous coating on

100# text

PURPOSE: To market

tattoos to people who

want to enhance their

tough-guy image.

AGENCY:

Jacobsen Advertising,

St. Louis, Missouri

CREATIVE DIRECTOR:

Brian C. Creath

ART DIRECTOR:

Shadrack Schoenke

PHOTOGRAPHER:

Stephen Kennedy

COPYWRITER: Frank Oros

BUDGET: $60,000

QUANTITY: 6 billboards

PRINTING PROCESS:

Silkscreen

PURPOSE: To re-establish

Volvo's safety image.

Volvo (Automotive)

Office of the Rhode Island Lieutenant Governor (Government Agency)

AGENCY:

Pagano Schenck & Kay,

Boston, Massachusetts

CREATIVE DIRECTOR:

Woody Kay

ART DIRECTOR:

Terry Rietta

ILLUSTRATOR: Eric Holter

COPYWRITER:

Bob Shiffrar

PURPOSE: To promote

awareness of the dangers

of lead poisoning.

DESIGN FIRM:
Royal Design,
Memphis, Tennessee
DESIGNER/ILLUSTRATOR:
Royal Design
PRINTING: Serigraphics
PAPER: Fox River Confetti
QUANTITY: 1000
PRINTING PROCESS:
5-color hand silkscreened
PURPOSE: To promote the
75th anniversary of the
oldest restaurant in
Memphis. Posters are sold
at the restaurant.

Arcade (Restaurant)

DESIGN FIRM:

Pentagram Design,

New York, New York

ART DIRECTOR/

DESIGNER: Paula Scher

PRINTER: Central Press

PAPER: Champion

Pageantry

PURPOSE: To promote a

talk by Paula Scher.

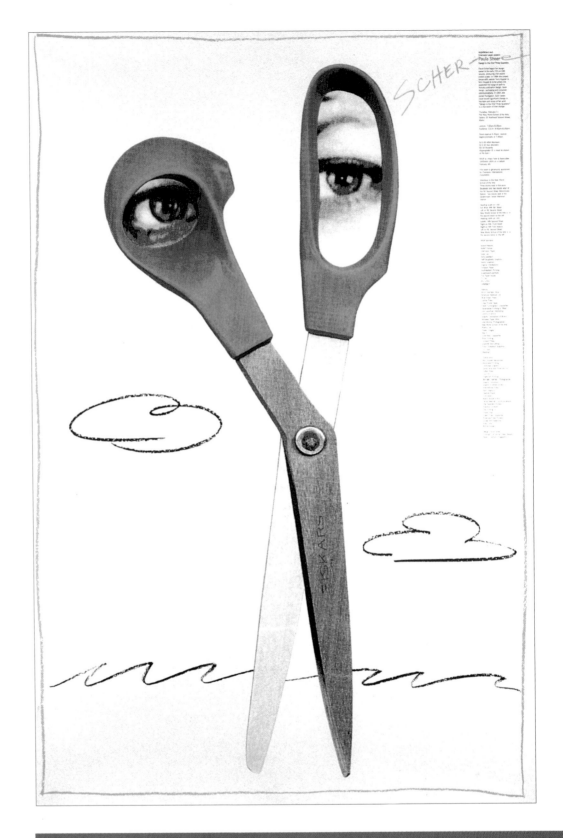

AIGA/Miami

WARNING: Paula Scher in Raleigh
Presented by AIGA, Sponsored by FGI
Thursday, February 24, 1994, 7:30pm
100 Hamilton Hall, University of
North Carolina, Chapel Hill

AIGA/Raleigh

DESIGN FIRM:

Pentagram Design,

New York, New York

ART DIRECTOR/

DESIGNER: Paul Scher

PHOTOGRAPHER:

John Paul Endress

PRINTER: Teagle & Little

PAPER: Finch Fine Smooth

PURPOSE: To promote a

talk by Paula Scher.

TO YOU IT'S A FRIENDLY GAME OF VOLLEYBALL. TO THEM IT'S ARMAGEDDON.

We didn't actually crush these Regal Fritillary Butterflies, just one of the 40 rare or endangered species of wildlife thriving on Block Island. And by calling us at 401-466-2129 we'll show you how to hike, bike and explore this extraordinary ecosystem without trampling any of its special inhabitants in the process.

 The Nature Conservancy

TO YOU IT'S A MOUNTAIN BIKE. TO THEM IT'S A STEAMROLLER.

Sure we didn't destroy this beautiful Bird's foot violet, just one of the 40 rare or endangered species that illustrates just how fragile ecosystem of Block Island. And if you call us at 401-466-2129 we'll show you how you how to hike, bike and explore this extraordinary island without plowing into this unique bottle, too.

 The Nature Conservancy

AGENCY:

Pagano Schenck & Kay, Boston, Massachusetts

CREATIVE DIRECTOR:

Woody Kay

ART DIRECTOR:

Robert Hamilton

ILLUSTRATOR:

Earl Bateman

COPYWRITER:

Steve Bautista

PURPOSE: Promotional

TO YOU IT'S A MORNING JOG. TO THEM IT'S A CLUSTER BOMB.

Of course, we didn't mean a good cause. You're not destroying these ants, just one of the 40 rare or endangered species of wildlife that inhabits the fragile ecosystem of Block Island. And by calling 401-466-2129 we will help you how to hike, bike and explore the island without running into this vulnerable bottle, too.

 The Nature Conservancy

BE SURE TO ASK ABOUT OUR TRAVEL INSURANCE.

NO CELLULAR PHONES, COMPUTERS OR VIDEO GAMES. LUCKY GUY.

STA Travel (Agency Specializing in Student Travel)

WHEN THE LAST PLACE ON EARTH IS EXACTLY WHERE YOU WANT TO BE.

SOMEHOW, CULTURAL BIAS AND PRECONCEIVED IDEAS JUST DON'T FIT IN A BACKPACK.

DESIGN FIRM: dGWB, Irvine, California

ART DIRECTOR: Wade Koniakowsky

DESIGNER: Mark Lyon

PHOTOGRAPHER: Rick Doyle

COPYWRITERS: Jim Real, Al Christiansen

BUDGET: $30,000

QUANTITY: 25 each of eight designs

PRINTING PROCESS: Large-format color output directly from disk (Digicolor)

PURPOSE: Point-of-purchase.

Twelfth Night

The Shakespeare Project *presents* Twelfth Night *or What You Will*, by Wm. Shakespeare. Admission is Free *Directed by* Scott Cargle. Our performances are; Central Park, Saturday June 11 at 11:00 PM and 4 PM. Sunday June 12 at 3:00 PM. Bryant Park. Sunday, June 19 and 26 at 3:00 PM. Fort Green Park, Brooklyn, Saturday, June 18 at 11:00 PM and 4:00 PM. and at The Henry Street Settlement. Abrons Art Center, Thursday, June 16 at 6:00 PM. Donations are greatly appreciated.

RICHARD III

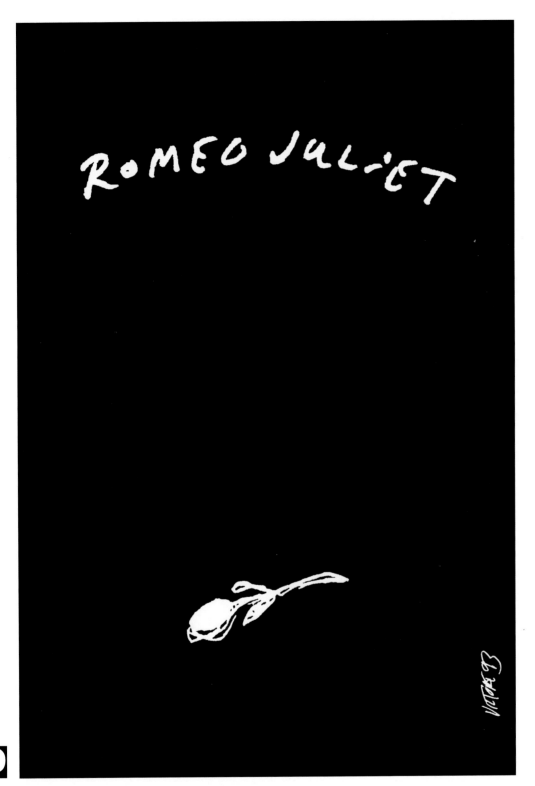

The Shakespeare Project

DESIGN FIRM:

Victore Design Works,

New York , New York

ART DIRECTOR:

James Victore

BUDGET: About $600 each

QUANTITY: 2000

PRINTING PROCESS:

Offset and silkscreen

PURPOSE: To promote

theater productions.

TWELFTH NIGHT
by William Shakespeare
Directed by
BARTLETT SHER
Sets designed by
DOUGLAS STEIN
Costumes designed by
KIM KRUMM SORENSON
Lighting designed by
DENNIS PARICHY
Music composed by
PETER STILL
Sound designed by
DEENA KAYE

THE ACTING COMPANY
All America's Our Stage
ZELDA FICHANDLER   MARGOT HARLEY
Artistic Director   Executive Producer

DESIGN FIRM:

Scott McKowen,

Lansing, Michigan

ART DIRECTOR/

DESIGNER/ILLUSTRATOR:

Scott McKowen

PRINTING PROCESS:

Offset lithography

reproduction of

scratchboard illustration

PURPOSE: To promote

national touring production

of Shakespeare's *Twelfth*

Night, performed in 30

cities across the U.S.

The Acting Company

A non-profit annual arts festival presenting hundreds of performance events and artists from around the world—the largest festival of its kind.

DESIGN FIRM:

Californiarol Hunt Design, Cleveland, Ohio

ART DIRECTOR:

Thomas Mulready

ILLUSTRATOR:

Deborah Palen

BUDGET: $10,000

QUANTITY: 15,000

PRINTING PROCESS:

Offset

PURPOSE: To promote the festival and serve as a schedule of events.

Page Education Foundation

An organization that helps to ensure an education for underprivileged children.

AGENCY:

Hoffman York & Compton, Milwaukee, Wisconsin

CREATIVE DIRECTOR:

Tom Jordan

ART DIRECTOR/

DESIGNER:

 Michael J. Wheaton

PHOTOGRAPHER:

Tim Waite

COPYWRITER:

Gene Payne

RETOUCHING:

Altered Images

QUANTITY: 1000

PURPOSE: To reinforce to kids the importance of an education as the best way to get ahead in life.

62

AGENCY:

GSD&M Advertising,

Austin, Texas

CREATIVE DIRECTORS:

Brent Ladd, Brian Brooker

ART DIRECTOR:

Scott McAfee

COPYWRITER: Tim Bauer

PHOTOGRAPHER:

Dennis Fagan

BUDGET: $8408.33

(donated labor valued at

$8237)

QUANTITY: 40,000

(30,000 in English,

10,000 in Spanish)

PRINTING PROCESS:

Black and gray duotone,

plus 1 PMS, plus varnish

PURPOSE: To prevent

inhalant abuse in pre-teens

and teens. Distributed to

public and private school

districts in Texas, civic

groups, mental health

organizations, and

community service

divisions.

SNIFFING SPRAY PAINT DESTROYS YOUR LUNGS.

Sniffing stuff like markers or spray paint can kill you. The first time, the second time, even the hundredth time. ⭐ Texas Prevention Partnership 1-800-269-4237

SNIFFING MARKERS DESTROYS YOUR BRAIN.

Sniffing stuff like spray paint or markers can cause brain damage, lung damage, even death. ⭐ Texas Prevention Partnership 1-800-269-4237

DESIGNER/ILLUSTRATOR:

Steven Rydberg,

New York, New York

BUDGET: $1500 (printing),

$1500 (fee)

QUANTITY: 1000 18" x 24"

posters, 3000 card mailers

PRINTING PROCESS:

4-color photo lithography

PURPOSE: To promote a

theater production; also

used as a give-away.

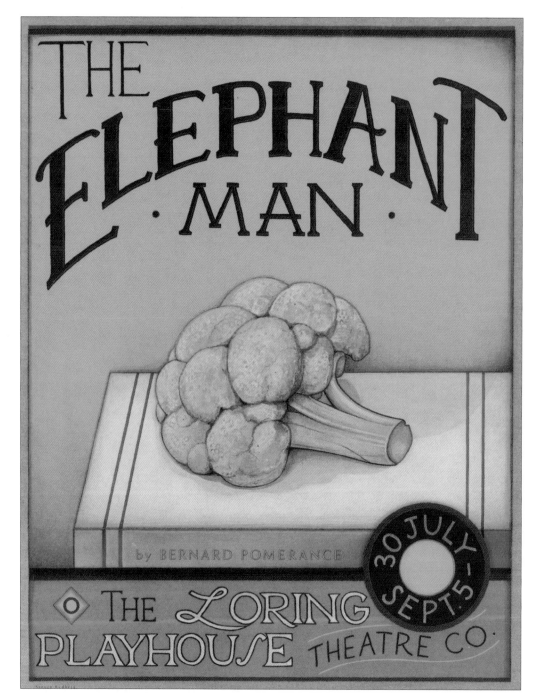

Loring Playhouse (Café/Bar/Theater)

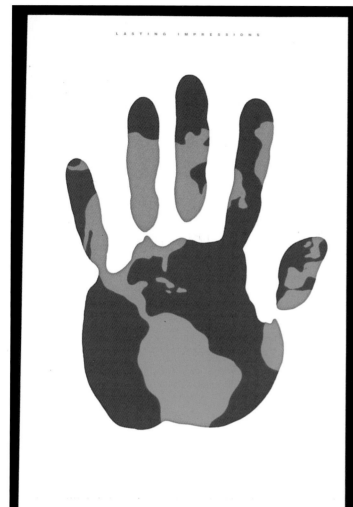

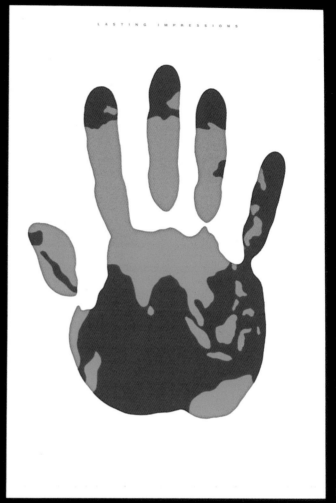

DESIGN FIRM:

Hill/A Marketing Design

Group, Houston, Texas

ART DIRECTOR: Chris Hill

ILLUSTRATORS:

Jeff Davis, Chris Hill

PRINTING PROCESS:

Silkscreen

PURPOSE: To promote an

exhibition about designers'

impact on the environment.

DESIGN FIRM:

Peter Good Graphic Design,

Chester, Connecticut

ART DIRECTOR/

DESIGNER: Peter Good

PURPOSE: To celebrate

opening of new patient

wing.

Photo by Jim Coon

This poster was specially produced to celebrate the opening of the new patient wing at Hospital for Special Care on October 5, 1993.

Hospital for Special Care

WE'LL HAVE BUDWEISER FOR THE PARENTS AND MILLER FOR THE STUDENTS.

DEATH OF A SALESMAN
ARTHUR MILLER

THE PROVIDENCE COUNTRY DAY SCHOOL
POT LUCK SUPPER & BOOK FAIR

Thursday, January 27, 7:00 p.m. Memorial Hall

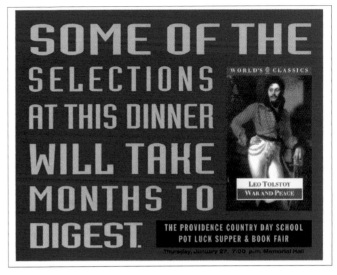

SOME OF THE SELECTIONS AT THIS DINNER WILL TAKE MONTHS TO DIGEST.

WORLD'S CLASSICS
LEO TOLSTOY
WAR AND PEACE

THE PROVIDENCE COUNTRY DAY SCHOOL
POT LUCK SUPPER & BOOK FAIR

Thursday, January 27, 7:00 p.m. Memorial Hall

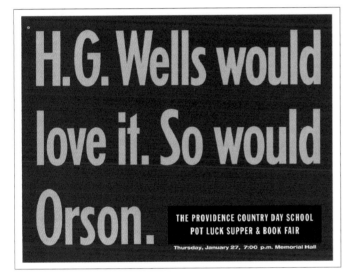

H.G. Wells would love it. So would Orson.

THE PROVIDENCE COUNTRY DAY SCHOOL
POT LUCK SUPPER & BOOK FAIR

Thursday, January 27, 7:00 p.m. Memorial Hall

Tonight's buffet will feature delicious pasta, fabulous chicken and great white whale.

HERMAN MELVILLE
MOBY DICK

THE PROVIDENCE COUNTRY DAY SCHOOL
POT LUCK SUPPER & BOOK FAIR

Thursday, January 27, 7:00 p.m. Memorial Hall

AGENCY:
Pagano Schenck & Kay,
Boston, Massachusetts

CREATIVE DIRECTOR:
Woody Kay

ART DIRECTOR:
Robert Hamilton

COPYWRITER: Tim Cawley

PURPOSE: To promote the
school's pot-luck supper
and book fair.

Providence Country Day School

AGENCY:
Young & Laramore,
Indianapolis, Indiana
CREATIVE DIRECTORS:
Jeff Laramore, David Young

ART DIRECTOR:
Chris Beatty
BUDGET: $2500
QUANTITY: 1
PRINTING PROCESS: Paint

PURPOSE: To create an identity and increase awareness of the product.

Red Gold Tomatoes

Postcards were also used to generate interest in the auction.

DESIGN FIRM: Tharp Did It,

Los Gatos, California

ART DIRECTOR: Rick Tharp

DESIGNERS: Rick Tharp,

Colleen Sullivan

ILLUSTRATOR:

Milton Glaser

COPYWRITER: Mark Fulton

LOGOTYPE:

Galarneau & Sinn

BUDGET: Pro bono

QUANTITY: 4000

PRINTING PROCESS:

4-color

PURPOSE: To promote

participation and

attendance at the

Miniature Art Auction, a

fundraiser for the club's

scholarship fund.

Western Art Directors Club

NUCLEAR PLANT
EXPERIENCE CONFERENCE
Forging Our Industry's Future
Sponsored by B&W Nuclear Technologies

Williamsburg, Virginia

© 1993 MICHAEL SCHWAB DESIGN

Developer/marketer of technologically advanced products and services for nuclear utilities, industry and goverment.

DESIGN FIRM:

Imagination By Design, Inc., Lynchburg, Virginia

ART DIRECTOR:

Larry Bevins

DESIGNER/ILLUSTRATOR:

Michael Schwab

CONSULTANTS:

Bill Warner, Richard Gentile/B&W Nuclear Technologies

PRINTER:

Overington Graphics

QUANTITY: 250

PRINTING PROCESS:

Silkscreen

PURPOSE: Promotional/ marketing device targeting upper-level executives. BWNT invites customers and friends from all over the world to attend a week-long conference held in Williamsburg, Virginia, every 18 months.

The Headless Horseman
of Sleepy Hollow

World Premiere
of Jon Deak's composition
based on Washington Irving's
American Classic.
Mstislav Rostropovich
conducting the
National Symphony Orchestra
and the Manchester String Quartet

Commissioned by the
Merck Company Foundation in 1991
in celebration of the centennial
of Merck & Co., Inc.

Manchester String Quartet:
Hyun-Woo Kim, violin
Jane Bowyer Stewart, violin
Nancy Thomas Bittner, viola
Glenn Garlick, cello

Kennedy Center Concert Hall

January 30 and February 1, 1992
8:30 pm

February 4, 1992
7:00 pm

DESIGN FIRM:
Peter Good Graphic Design,
Chester, Connecticut
ART DIRECTOR/
DESIGNER/ILLUSTRATOR:
Peter Good
PURPOSE: To promote
world premiere of musical
work commissioned for
Merck's centennial
celebration.

OUT OF ALL THE WEAPONS USED TO FIGHT RELIGIOUS WARS, ONLY ONE HAS PROVED SUCCESSFUL.

Jefferson's Statute for Religious Freedom established, for the first time, that an individual's conscience is a natural right beyond government control. It gave us religious freedom and for 200 years religious peace. Help us build a home for it at the site of its birth, here in Richmond at 14th and Cary Streets. Call 804-643-1786.

Center For America's First Freedom.

Organization promoting religious freedom.

AGENCY:

The Martin Agency, Richmond, Virginia

ART DIRECTOR: Hal Tench

COPYWRITER:

John Mahoney

PHOTOGRAPHER:

Dean Hawthorne

PRINT PRODUCER:

Karen Smith

ACCOUNT EXECUTIVE:

Matt Thornhill

PRINTING PROCESS:

4-color plus spot dull varnish

PURPOSE: To solicit funds and state the purpose of the organization.

ONE BLACK VICTIM. ONE WHITE VICTIM. IS THIS WHAT RACIAL EQUALITY MEANS NOW?

If we don't begin to build trusting relationships between the races, what you see isn't the past of one American city, it's the future of all of them. Join us for an honest conversation on race, reconciliation and responsibility at a special National Cities Conference, June 16-20 at the Richmond Centre, Richmond, Virginia. Call 804-648-4216.

HEALING THE HEART OF AMERICA CONFERENCE

A racial equality conference held during a special National Cities Conference.

AGENCY:

The Martin Agency, Richmond , Virginia

ART DIRECTOR:

Mark Fuller

COPYWRITER:

John Mahoney

PRINT PRODUCER:

Melissa Ralston

BUDGET: $1000 donated by printer, plus agency donation of $1072

QUANTITY: 2000

PRINTING PROCESS:

1-color lithography

PURPOSE: To publicize the date and purpose of the conference and the sponsoring organization.

AGENCY:

Sive/Young & Rubicam,

Cincinnati, Ohio

CREATIVE DIRECTOR:

Mike Kitei

ART DIRECTOR: Clifton Lin

ILLUSTRATOR:

Jeffrey Terreson

COPYWRITER:

Bruce Carlson

PRINT PRODUCTION

MANAGERS:

George Noltensmeyer,

Steve Jones

ACCOUNT EXECUTIVE:

Linda Jackson

Bears. Imagination and Reality.
🏛 CINCINNATI MUSEUM OF NATURAL HISTORY, MUSEUM CENTER

This Time, No Teddy Bears.
🏛 CINCINNATI MUSEUM OF NATURAL HISTORY

AGENCY: Evans Group,

Salt Lake City, Utah

ART DIRECTOR:

Steve Cardon

DESIGNER/ILLUSTRATOR:

McRay Magleby

COPYWRITER:

John Kinkead

PURPOSE: Promotional

transit ad.

DESIGN FIRM:

Modern Dog,

Seattle, Washington

ART DIRECTOR:

Robynne Raye, Dan Ripley

DESIGNER/ILLUSTRATOR:

Robynne Raye

BUDGET: Pro bono

QUANTITY: 350

PRINTING PROCESS:

Screenprinting

PURPOSE: To inform and

educate the public about

the project.

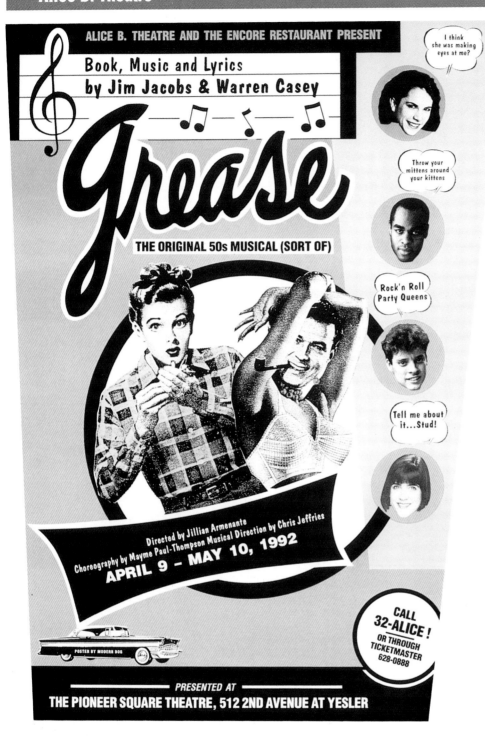

DESIGN FIRM:

Modern Dog,

Seattle , Washington

ART DIRECTORS:

Michael Strassburger,

Vittorio Costarella

BUDGET: $650

(printing only)

QUANTITY: 350

PRINTING PROCESS:

Offset

PURPOSE: To promote a

theatrical production.

Professional association of designers in Madison, Wisconsin.

DESIGN FIRM:
Pentagram Design,
New York, New York

ART DIRECTOR/
DESIGNER/ILLUSTRATOR:
Woody Pirtle

PURPOSE: To promote a talk by Woody Pirtle.

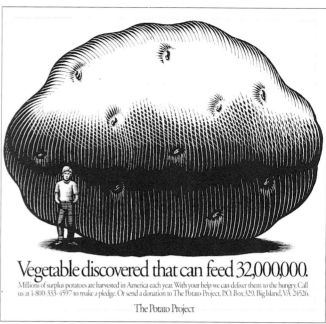

Vegetable discovered that can feed 32,000,000.

Millions of surplus potatoes are harvested in America each year. With your help we can deliver them to the hungry. Call us at 1-800-333-4597 to make a pledge. Or send a donation to The Potato Project, P.O. Box 329, Big Island, VA 24526.

The Potato Project

Society of St. Andrews/The Potato Project

AGENCY:

The Martin Agency,

Richmond, Virginia

ART DIRECTOR:

Shari Hindman

ILLUSTRATOR:

Mark Weakley

COPYWRITER:

Raymond McKinney

PRINT PRODUCER:

Jenny Schoenherr

ACCOUNT EXECUTIVE:

Matt Thornhill

BUDGET: $1500 paid by

client and $1500 paid by

supplier

QUANTITY: 1000 each

PRINTING PROCESS:

Sheet-fed 1-color on

Speckeltone Madero

Beach White 80# cover

PURPOSE: To raise

money and awareness for

the Potato Project, an

organization that takes

food that ordinarily would

go to waste and

transports it to the needy.

In 1845, thousands died during the potato famine. Today, the potato is ready to redeem itself.

Unlike Ireland in the mid 1800's, America has millions of surplus potatoes. With your help we can deliver them to the hungry. Call us at 1-800-333-4597 to make a pledge. Or send a donation to The Potato Project, P.O. Box 329, Big Island, VA 24526.

The Potato Project

Midnight Blue by Michael Hart

Fire Red by Ken Childress

Forest Green by Arthur Meyerson

DESIGN FIRM:
Dwight Douthit Design,
Houston, Texas
ART DIRECTOR/
DESIGNER: Dwight Douthit
COPYWRITER:
Paula Randall
PHOTOGRAPHERS:
Michael Hart (Midnight
Blue), Ken Childress (Fire
Red), Arthur Meyerson
(Forest Green), Terry Vine
(Harvest Gold), Raymond
Groscrand (Peaches),
Terry Asker (Crystal Blue)
QUANTITY: 5000
PRINTING PROCESS:
Heidelberg 6-color
lithography
PURPOSE: To promote
a new color and prepress
division of Brandt &
Lawson

Harvest Gold by Terry Line

Paper: 100 lb.
Line Line/Dot
Not available at
Bond & Lorien

Soft Peach by Raymond Genestrand

Paper: 100 lb.
Line Line/Dot
Not available at
Bond & Lorien

Crystal Blue by Terry Eden

Paper: 100 lb.
Line Line/Dot
Not available at
Bond & Lorien

AGENCY: Evans Group,

Salt Lake City, Utah

ART DIRECTOR/

DESIGNER: Dick Brown

PHOTOGRAPHER:

Steve Bunderson

COPYWRITER:

Rebecca Bentley-Mila

PURPOSE: Public-service

billboards about the

effects of drinking on

driving.

Gus Paulos Chevrolet (Automotive)

DESIGN FIRM:

Lawrence & Mayo,

Newport Beach, California

ART DIRECTORS:

Bruce Mayo, Kinsey Caruth

DESIGNERS: Bruce Mayo,

Lisa Dietzel

PHOTOGRAPHER:

Tom Hollar

COPYWRITER:

Lynda Lawrence

PURPOSE: To increase

awareness of AIDS hot-line

*Below: foldout brochure;
bottom, right: bus shelter
transit ad; bottom, far right:
promotional mailer.*

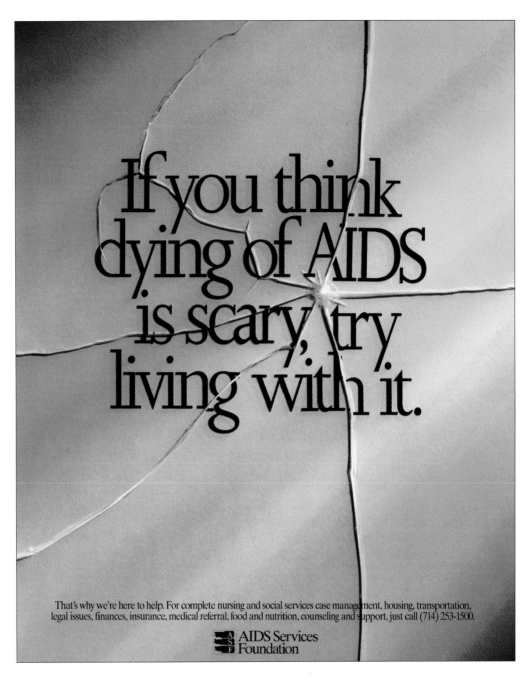

AIDS Services Foundation (AIDS Support Group)

DESIGN FIRM:

Icehouse Press,

Atlanta, Georgia

ART DIRECTORS:

Bjorn Akselsen,

Pattie Belle Hastings

DESIGNER/ILLUSTRATOR:

Bjorn Akselsen

BUDGET: $2000

QUANTITY: 750

PRINTING PROCESS:

2-color offset

PURPOSE: To attract

submissions to a Georgia

high school drawing

competition and exhibition

hosted by the college.

DESIGN FIRM: dGWB,

Irvine, California

ART DIRECTOR:

Lee Calderon

PHOTOGRAPHER:

William Hawkes

COPYWRITER:

Al Christiansen

BUDGET: $25,000

QUANTITY: 500

PRINTING PROCESS:

4-color offset

PURPOSE: Promotional

give-away

AGENCY:

The Martin Agency,

Richmond, Virginia

ART DIRECTOR:

Bob Meagher

PHOTOGRAPHERS:

Mark Scott,

Dean Hawthorne

(Shadow Canyon)

COPYWRITER:

Joe Alexander (Shadow

Canyon), Steve Dolbinski

(Checotah)

PRINT PRODUCER:

Jenny Schoenherr

ACCOUNT EXECUTIVE:

Ann Henley

BUDGET: $9625

QUANTITY: 2500

PRINTING PROCESS:

Sheet-fed 4-color plus

aqueous coating on 100#

text

PURPOSE: To introduce

western jeans and shirts

collections.

AGENCY:

The Martin Agency, Richmond, Virginia

ART DIRECTOR:

Shari Hindman

PHOTOGRAPHER:

Tony Sylvestro

COPYWRITER:

Steve Doblinski

PRINT PRODUCER:

Karen Smith

ACCOUNT EXECUTIVE:

Kevin Best

BUDGET: Printer donated $2150

QUANTITY: 300

PRINTING PROCESS: Double-dot black with spot color, plus dull varnish

PURPOSE: To encourage women to volunteer time to the Girl Scouts.

Help a young woman discover there are no limits to what she can do. Please volunteer your time to the Girl Scouts by calling the Commonwealth Girl Scout Council at (804) 746-0590.

Provide an environment for a young woman where the only thing being promoted is personal development. Please volunteer your time to the Girl Scouts by calling the Commonwealth Girl Scout Council at (804) 746-0590.

DECEPTION. TRICKERY. ARTIFICIAL INGREDIENTS. THINGS YOU BUILD A BUSINESS ON.

WHEN WE STARTED THE BUSINESS, YOU COULD ALMOST HEAR THE TROUT LAUGHING.

WHY NOT START A BUSINESS? WE ALREADY HAD THE OFFICE EQUIPMENT.

WHAT HUCK FINN WOULD'VE DONE, IF HE'D GONE TO HARVARD BUSINESS SCHOOL.

AGENCY:

The Martin Agency,

Richmond, Virginia

ART DIRECTOR:

Mark Fuller

PHOTOGRAPHER:

Tony Sylvestro

COPYWRITER:

John Mahoney

PRINT PRODUCER:

Jenny Schoenherr

BUDGET: $5000 supplier

donated

QUANTITY: 750

PRINTING PROCESS:

Sheet-fed 4-color plus

aqueous coating on 100#

matte cover

PURPOSE: To promote the

company's function and

image.

Farm at Mt. Walden (Smoked Fish Farm)

Howard's Soup Kitchen (Soup/Sandwich Restaurant)

AGENCY:

The Packett Group,

Roanoke, Virginia

ART DIRECTOR:

Shawn Murray

COPYWRITERS:

Lane Foard, Robin Chalkley

BUDGET: $500 for posters

QUANTITY: 200 each

PRINTING PROCESS:

Offset

PURPOSE: To announce

the opening of a restaurant,

and to get the most impact

out of a very small budget.

Above: Sandwich board worn on streets surrounding the restaurant during the first week; left: front and back of take-out bag includes a menu.

DESIGN FIRM:

Martin/Williams,

Minneapolis, Minnesota

DESIGNER: Robb Burnham

COPYWRITER: Chris Wilson

PURPOSE: To encourage

alumni to attend a class

reunion.

DESIGN FIRM:

Joseph Rattan Design,

Dallas, Texas

ART DIRECTOR: Joe Rattan

DESIGNER: Greg Morgan

ILLUSTRATOR:

Linda Helton

BUDGET: Pro bono

QUANTITY: 2000

PRINTING PROCESS:

4-color, sheet-fed

PURPOSE: Announcement

of, and invitation to,

seminar.

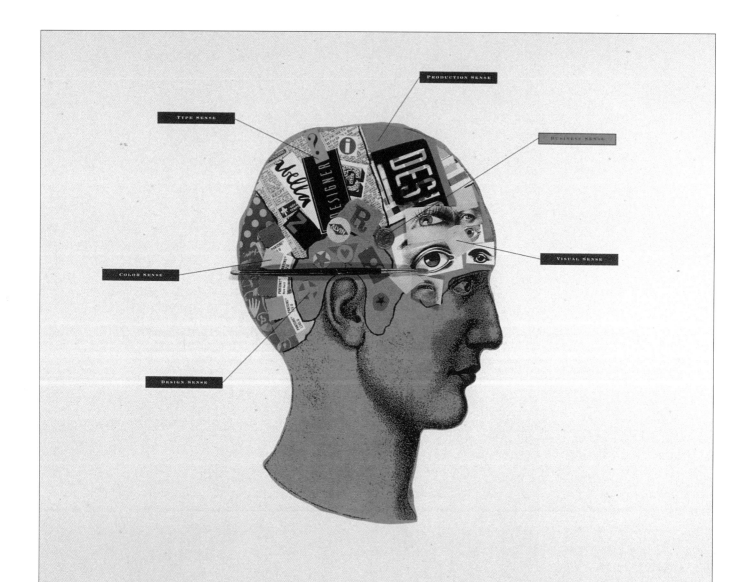

U S E   S O M E   C O M M O N   S E N S E.

ATTEND THE AIGA TEXAS BUSINESS OF GRAPHIC DESIGN SEMINAR. FRIDAY, MAY 14, 1993, 9AM-5PM. CITYPLACE CONFERENCE CENTER, JOE C. THOMPSON
AMPHITHEATER. ONE MILE SOUTH OF DOWNTOWN ON I-75 (CENTRAL EXPRESSWAY) AT 2711 NORTH HASKELL AVENUE, DALLAS, TEXAS.

DESIGN FIRM:

Atelier Design, Inc.,

Washington, DC

ART DIRECTOR/

DESIGNER/ILLUSTRATOR:

Pete Beebe

QUANTITY: 15

PRINTING PROCESS: IRIS

print on Rieves 100%

cotton rag printmaking

paper

PURPOSE: To display on

tables and around the

interior of the café.

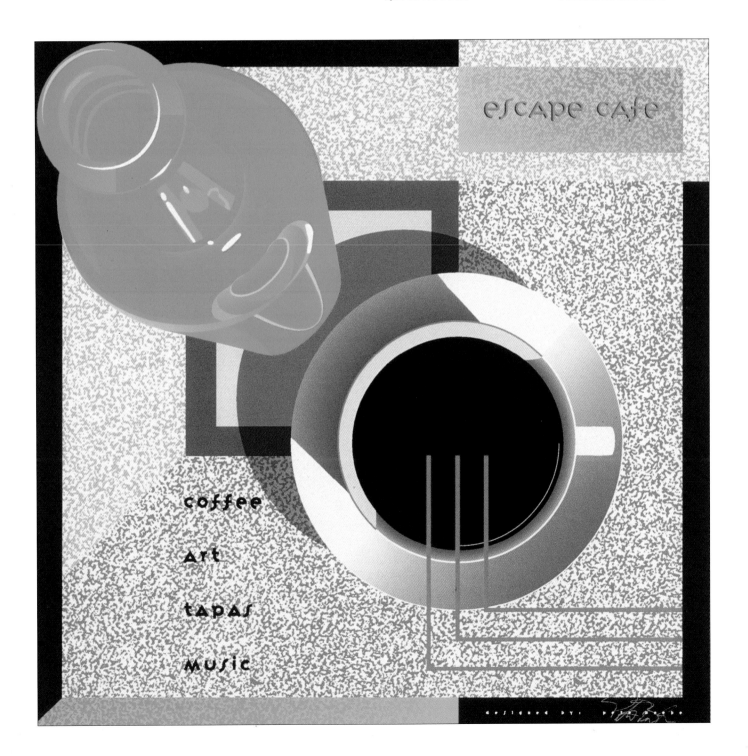

Gather ye rosebuds while ye may
Old Time is still a-flying;
And this same flower that smiles today
Tomorrow will be dying.

Heed not the passing planting season
Use it well or
You'll end with good reason
Fall to better regeneration
in cutting August 15

N EITHER A PALLID WALLFLOWER NOR A PANSY BE,
NOR FOUND WILTED BY THE CRUEL BREATH OF TIME
A FORLORN LATE BLOOMER LEFT HANGING ON THE VINE
BE ONE WHO ROSE TO THE OCCASION FULL-FLOWERED,
BY PROMPT REGISTRATION CONSUMMATELY EMPOWERED
TUITION PAYMENT DEADLINE FOR SUMMER TERM-JUNE 11

ART DIRECTOR:

McRay Magleby,

University Publications,

Provo, Utah

DESIGNERS:

McRay Magleby, Lily

McCullough (Wallflowers)

SILKSCREENER:

Rory Robinson

PURPOSE: To encourage

early registration.

SOME SEE THE WORLD OF BUSINESS AS DOG EAT DOG.

AT BYU'S MARRIOTT SCHOOL OF MANAGEMENT

STUDENTS SEE A WORLD OF OPPORTUNITY.

O pportunities abound for exciting and rewarding careers upon completion of a Marriott School professional degree: the Master of Business Administration (MBA), Master of Public Administration (MPA), Master of Accountancy (MAcc), or Master of Organizational Behavior (MOB). An advanced degree from the Marriott School of Management means proficiency in a broad range of management skills and professional attributes that ensure career success.

Programs emphasize integration across functional areas, breadth in course work, exposure to behavioral aspects of management, oral and written communication skills, and the critical ability to keep abreast of the changing world of management. In addition, the school's atmosphere is truly international—more than 80 percent of its students are bilingual.

FACULTY MEMBERS ARE COMMITTED TO—
• educating students with the ethical values and unsurpassed management and leadership skills needed for today's international business economy,
• challenging students to engage in independent, entrepreneurial thinking and keep abreast of innovative research and techniques, and
• fostering an attitude of service and responsibility toward society.

At BYU, everything combines to enhance your graduate study experience and expand your career opportunities upon graduation.

For more information about BYU's Marriott School graduate management programs, please contact:

Marriott School of Management Graduate Programs

Brigham Young University

730 Tanner Building, Provo, Utah 84602

Telephone (801) 378-4123

ART DIRECTOR:

McRay Magleby,

University Publications,

Provo, Utah

DESIGNERS:

McRay Magleby,

Dave Eliason

PHOTOGRAPHER:

John Snyder

SILKSCREENER:

Rory Robinson

PURPOSE: Promotional

DESIGN FIRM:

Robin Shepherd Studios,

Jacksonville, Florida

DESIGNER/ILLUSTRATOR:

Tom Schifanella

PRINTER: Jonathan Cox

BUDGET: $600

QUANTITY: 100

PRINTING PROCESS:

Silkscreen

PURPOSE: To announce an

annual concert at the

University of North Florida.

AGENCY:

The Smart Guy's Advertising

Company, Huntington

Beach, California

ART DIRECTORS/

COPYWRITERS:

Pat Zimmerman,

Tim O'Donnell

DESIGNER: Pat Zimmerman

SEPARATOR/PRINTER:

On-line Imaging

BUDGET: $85,000

including envelopes

QUANTITY:

10,000–75,000 per poster

PURPOSE: Direct-mail

promotion to introduce

new hi-tech chips.

We know exactly what you want. It's inside. Are you saying to yourself, "Self, how can they know?" Don't worry about it, we know. And stop talking to yourself.

The mere thought of the personal gratification that lies within this envelope may very well singe your fingertips.

Only this envelope lies between you and destiny. Don't become a pathetic waste of human flesh! Quick, hurry, open it.

Left: direct-mail envelopes for
each of the posters.

UNTIL THEN.

Kurt's Land Mine Removal Service
FOR THE TIMES WHEN MAN'S BEST FRIEND ISN'T YOURS. 310.519.5328

**WE'RE REALLY
A LOT MORE PRACTICAL.**

Kurt's Land Mine Removal Service
FOR THE TIMES WHEN MAN'S BEST FRIEND ISN'T YOURS. 310.519.5328

**THERE'S NOTHING LIKE
A BAREFOOT WALK
THROUGH THE BACKYARD,
THE BREEZE AT YOUR
BACK, THE MOONLIGHT
CARESSING YOUR EVERY
MOVE AND THE WARMTH
OF A FRESH TURD
SQUISHING BETWEEN
YOUR TOES.**

Kurt's Land Mine Removal Service
FOR THE TIMES WHEN MAN'S BEST FRIEND ISN'T YOURS. 310.519.5328

AGENCY:

The Smart Guy's Advertising

Company, Huntington

Beach, California

ART DIRECTORS/

COPYWRITERS:

Pat Zimmerman,

Tim O'Donnell

DESIGNER: Pat Zimmerman

PHOTOGRAPHER:

Paul Taylor

PRINTER: Loy Litho

BUDGET: $4000

QUANTITY: 200

PRINTING PROCESS:

Offset

PURPOSE: To promote a

dog poop removal service;

displayed at vet offices and

pet supply stores and used

for direct mail.

Non-profit, artist-run organization dedicated to the development of a strong art community in downtown Phoenix.

DESIGN FIRM: Estudio Ray, Scottsdale, Arizona

ART DIRECTORS/ DESIGNERS: Joe Ray, Christine Ray

ILLUSTRATOR: Joe Ray

PRINTER: Heritage Graphics

COLOR SEPARATOR: Laserscan, Inc.

PAPER: Potlatch Quintessence, 80# dull cover

BUDGET: Pro bono

QUANTITY: 35,000

PRINTING PROCESS: 4-color

PURPOSE: To let people know of the upcoming Art Detour of Studios in downtown Phoenix.

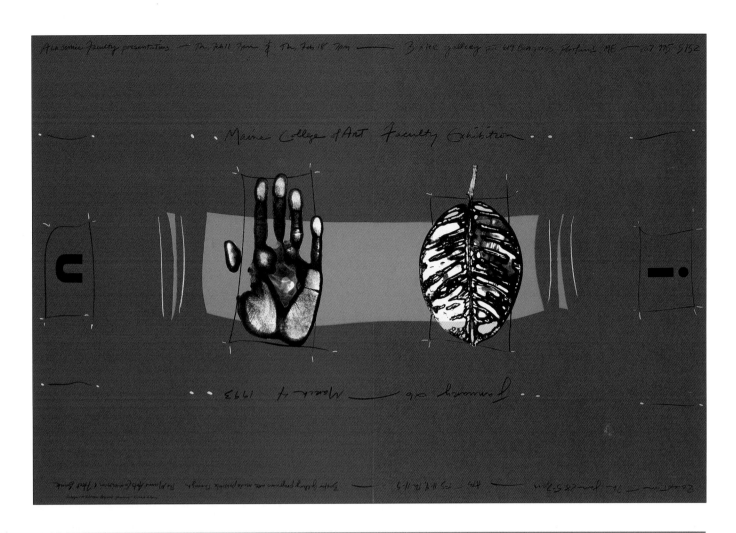

DESIGN FIRM:

Halverson Graphic Design,

Portland, Maine

ART DIRECTOR/

DESIGNER:

Margo Halverson

PRODUCTION:

Richard Wilson

BUDGET: $500 for printing

and paper, design time

donated

QUANTITY: 100

PRINTING PROCESS:

Silkscreen

PURPOSE: To promote

1993 faculty exhibition.

This is one of a series of

silkscreen handprints—

hand ideas— done each

year for the exhibition.

AGENCY:

Thompson & Company,

Memphis, Tennessee

CREATIVE DIRECTORS:

Trace Hallowell,

Michael H. Thompson

ART DIRECTOR/

DESIGNER/COPYWRITER:

Bill Ainsworth

ILLUSTRATOR:

Danny Smythe

BUDGET: Pro bono

QUANTITY: 500

PRINTING PROCESS:

4-color

PURPOSE: To announce

the annual symphony

fundraiser ball and that

year's nautical theme.

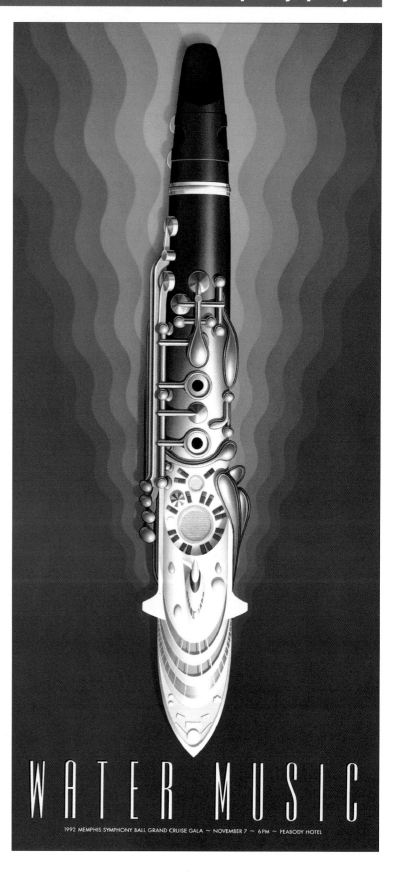

DESIGN FIRM:

Dye Van Mol & Lawrence,

Nashville, Tennessee

CREATIVE DIRECTOR:

Chuck Creasy

ART DIRECTOR/

DESIGNER: Gregg Boling

PHOTOGRAPHER:

Michael W. Rutherford

COPYWRITER:

Tracy Johnson

BUDGET: Under $5000

QUANTITY: 1500

PRINTING PROCESS: 300

line screen, 4-color plus

5th and 6th color touch

plates, aqueous coated

PURPOSE: Poster was

printed and distributed at

an open house to

demonstrate capabilities.

Above: a series of teaser postcards inviting potential clients to an open house.

DESIGN FIRM:

Hunt Murray,

Minneapolis, Minnesota

ART DIRECTOR:

Mike Fetrow

ILLUSTRATOR:

Mitch Sondreaal

PHOTOGRAPHER:

Shawn Michienzi

COPYWRITER:

Doug Adkins

DESIGN FIRM:

Farnet Hart Design,

New Orleans, Louisiana

ART DIRECTOR/

DESIGNER: Winnie Hart

PHOTOGRAPHER:

William Guion

PURPOSE: Promotional

OAKS IN FOG, MANRESA RETREAT, 1990

THE LIGHT AROUND THE OAKS

PHOTOGRAPHS BY WILLIAM GUION

A PORTFOLIO OF PHOTOGRAPHS OF LIVE OAK TREES OF LOUISIANA AND THE SOUTH

Merci beaucoup to Winnie Hart, Hartax Design for poster design; printed by Pat Elwick, Crown Stirling International Printers, New Orleans; double-black duotone, with varnish coat; 200-line laser-scanned duotone separation by Hanson Graphics, New Orleans; paper from Marks Paper Co., Quintessence Dull, 80 lb. cover. For portfolio purchase information, contact William Guion, (504) 366-4718.

DESIGN FIRM:

Mires Design,

San Diego, California

ART DIRECTOR:

José Serrano

DESIGNER: José Serrano

ILLUSTRATOR: Tracy

Sabin (Park Bench truck)

PHOTOGRAPHER:

Chris Wimpey (People

Reading truck)

QUANTITY: 1

PRINTING PROCESS:

3M Scotchprint

PURPOSE: Promotional

THE NEW HILLTOP YMCA. THERE'S SOMETHING GOING ON HERE.

*Below: Three bus shelter
designs used in the campaign.*

THE NEW HILLTOP YMCA.
THERE'S SOMETHING GOING ON HERE.

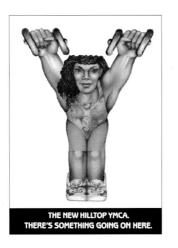

THE NEW HILLTOP YMCA.
THERE'S SOMETHING GOING ON HERE.

THE NEW HILLTOP YMCA.
THERE'S SOMETHING GOING ON HERE.

AGENCY:

Hal Riney & Partners,

San Francisco, California

ART DIRECTOR/

DESIGNER: Chris Chaffin

ILLUSTRATOR:

Jozef Sumichrast

BUDGET: $10,000

PURPOSE: To introduce

the new Hilltop YMCA to

the residents of

Richmond, California.

Photo by Will Shively

DESIGN FIRM:

Firehouse 101 Design,

Columbus, Ohio

ART DIRECTOR/

DESIGNER/

CALLIGRAPHER:

Kirk Richard Smith

CREATIVE CONTRIBUTOR:

Charles Wagner

PHOTOGRAPHER:

Steven Webster

PRINTER: Southprint

FILM: Dwight Yaeger

BUDGET: Pro bono

QUANTITY: 800

PRINTING PROCESS:

1-color

PURPOSE: To create a

poster based on people's

personal dreams as the

copy and imagery within

the poster. A flyer

explaining the project and

giving a call-in phone

number to record the

caller's dream was

distributed to shopping

malls, restaurants, and

bars in various city

neighborhoods.

Columbus Society of Communicating Arts

Politics

AND THE HUMAN BODY

A Conference of the Vanderbilt University Program in Social and Political Thought

January 22 and 23, 1993
Wilson Hall 103
Vanderbilt University

Sponsored by the Program in Social and Political Thought, the University Research Council, the Office of University Relations, the School of Medicine, the Vanderbilt University Medical Center, and the Andrew Woodfin Miller Foundation.

CONSIDER
THE PROGRAM IN SOCIAL AND POLITICAL THOUGHT

A conference bringing together a distinguished group of political philosophers, theologians, ethicists, scientists, legal theorists, medical practitioners, business leaders, and media figures to analyze many complex features of the human body and politics as we enter the twenty-first century. These include pain, suffering, death, euthanasia, genetic engineering, health care costs and coverage, discipline, torture as a political instrument, and cultural images of the body.

Who makes decisions about life and death?
Are real choices involved?
Who has a voice? The government? Doctors? The health care industry? Families? Feminists? Scientists? The media?
What are our cultural images of the body?
How does the new science and technology of the body alter our views of the human community and the "body politic?"
New reproductive technologies—boon or bane?
Is the human body abused and misused culturally and politically?
Have attitudes about persons with disabilities and the "perfect body" changed?
How does our culture deny death?

KEYNOTE EVENT
Friday, January 22
12–1 p.m.
Sarratt Cinema
Frederick Wiseman

KEYNOTE PANEL
Friday, January 22
4–6 p.m.
Wilson Hall 103
Richard Lewontin
Gilbert Meilaender
Orlando Patterson
Stanley Hauerwas
Eric Cassell
Jean Bethke Elshtain

FIVE PANEL SERIES AND RECEPTION
Saturday, January 23
9–7 p.m.
Wilson Hall 103

PANEL ONE
Pain, Suffering, and Death
9–10:30 a.m.
PANEL TWO
Cultural Images of the Body
10:45 a.m.–12:15 p.m.
PANEL THREE
Reproductive Technologies
1–2:30 p.m.
PANEL FOUR
Dollars, Cents, and Death
2:45–4:15 p.m.
PANEL FIVE
Discipline, Punishment, and Torture
4:30–6 p.m.
PUBLIC RECEPTION
6–7 p.m.

ASSAULT ON DIGNITY

Vanderbilt University is committed to principles of equal opportunity and affirmative action. Published by University Publications and Design, 1992.

DESIGNER/ILLUSTRATOR: Tom Ventress, Vanderbilt University Publications and Design, Nashville, Tennessee

EDITOR/WRITER: Gregory Fisher

BUDGET: $1350

QUANTITY: 3500

PRINTING PROCESS: Offset; black, PMS 485 red, PMS 467 tan

PURPOSE: To publicize a conference bringing together a group of political philosophers, theologians, ethicists, scientists, legal theorists, medical practitioners, business leaders, and media figures to discuss the theme of "Politics and the Human Body."

DESIGN FIRM:

Bartels & Company, Inc.,

St. Louis, Missouri

ART DIRECTION:

David Bartels

ILLUSTRATOR:

James Grashow

BUDGET: $10,000

QUANTITY: 3000

PRINTING PROCESS:

2-color lithography

PURPOSE: To announce a

client's participation in a

tradeshow; also used as a

tradeshow give-away.

GIS IN BUSINESS   BOSTON 1993

TAKING CHARGE OF BUSINESS

WITH THE WRONG MAP, THIS COULD BE THE ROAD TO NOWHERE.

AN EDS PRODUCT

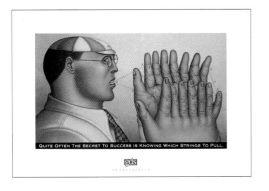

QUITE OFTEN THE SECRET TO SUCCESS IS KNOWING WHICH STRINGS TO PULL.

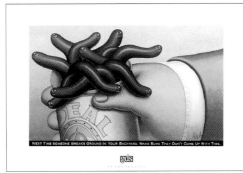

NEXT TIME SOMEONE BREAKS GROUND IN YOUR BACKYARD. MAKE SURE THEY DON'T COME UP WITH THIS.

DESIGN FIRM:

Bartels & Company, Inc.,

St. Louis, Missouri

ART DIRECTION:

David Bartels

ILLUSTRATORS:

Mark Ryden (Road to

Nowhere), Roy

Carruthers (Secret to

Success, Can of Worms)

BUDGET: $10,000

QUANTITY: 3000

PRINTING PROCESS:

6-color lithography

PURPOSE: Premium for a

trade magazine campaign.

ART DIRECTOR/
DESIGNER: Steven Rydberg,
Libertyville, Illinois
PURPOSE:
To commemorate the
restaurant's 10th
anniversary.

DESIGN FIRM:

Robin Shepherd Studios,

Jacksonville, Florida

DESIGNER/ILLUSTRATOR:

Tom Schifanella

COPYWRITER: Bob White

PRINTER: Jonathan Cox

BUDGET: $600

QUANTITY: 100

PRINTING PROCESS:

Silkscreen

PURPOSE: To promote a

theatrical production. A

paint roller was used to

produce the random border

at the edges.

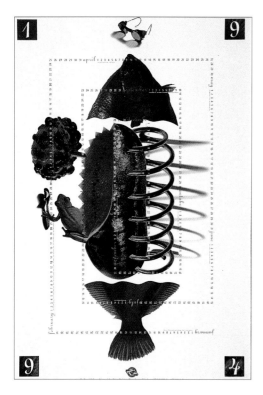

DESIGN FIRM:

Encompass

Communications, Inc. ,

Boston , Massachusetts

ART DIRECTOR: I Jian Lin

DESIGNERS: I Jian Lin,

Martin Sorger

PHOTOGRAPHER:

Francine Zaslow

QUANTITY: 2500

PRINTING PROCESS:

4-color with 4 bump colors

plus four metallics plus

two varnishes

PURPOSE: Promotional

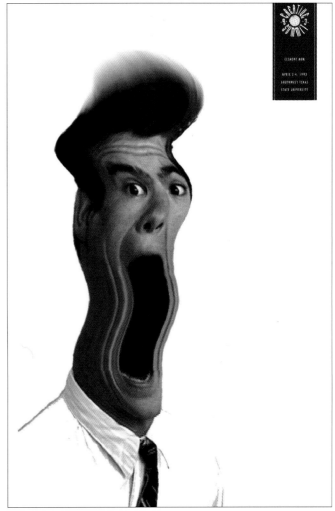

Left and above, right: other give-away pieces in the promotion.

ART DIRECTORS:

William Meek/Southwest

Texas State University,

San Marcos, Texas;

Chris Hill/The Hill Group

DESIGNER: Jeff Davis

ILLUSTRATOR:

J. Otto Seibold

PRINTER: Padgett Printing

BUDGET: Pro bono

QUANTITY: 500

PRINTING PROCESS:

4-color plus varnish

PURPOSE: Give-away at the

1993 design conference.

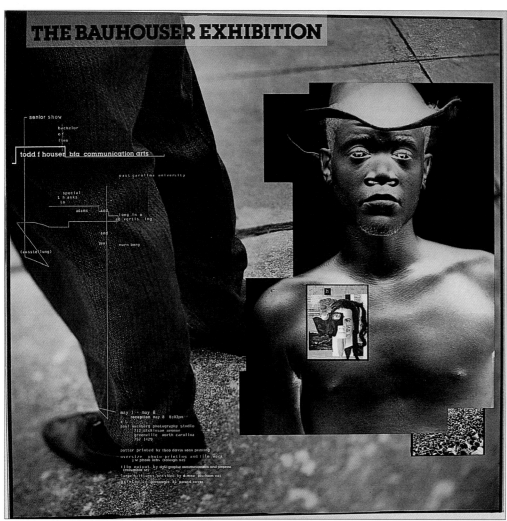

THE BAUHOUSER EXHIBITION

senior show
bachelor
of
fine
todd f houser bfa communication arts

east carolina university

special
thanks
to
adams and longino advertising

and
paul nuremberg

(ausstellung)

may 1 - may 8
reception may 8 8:03pm
at
paul nuremberg photography studio
712 dickinson avenue
greenville north carolina
757 1429

poster printed by theo davis sons printing
oversize photo printing and film work
| w photo labs (raleigh nc)
film output by dgitgraphic communications and prepress
(columbia sc)
large multilines provided by 0-max (durham nc)
printed on gleneagle 65 pound cover

ART DIRECTOR/
DESIGNER/
PHOTOGRAPHER:
Todd Houser, Miami, Florida
PRINTER: Theo Davis Sons
BUDGET: $250 plus a
tradeout with the printer
QUANTITY: 500
PRINTING PROCESS:
3-color plus spot varnish,
offset, sheet-fed
PURPOSE: To announce
Houser's senior exhibition
at East Carolina University;
then used as a self-
promotion piece when he
began looking for a job.

Todd Houser

INTERVIEW
INTERVIEW
INTERVIEW
?

richard steven bean
memorial scholarship
for graphic design

internship
h at
adams and longino
advertising

seven addy award [including best in show]
dean's list/honor roll
1990-1993

I am graduating this spring (1993)
with a BFA in communication arts
from East Carolina University.
I would like the opportunity
to interview with your firm,
show you my portfolio, and discuss
possible employment.

Thank you.

todd f houser

919 355 6883

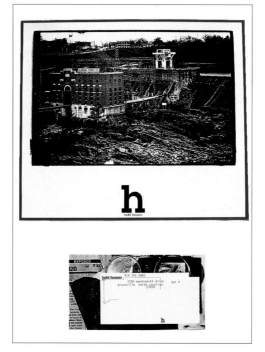

Far left: partial resumé / interview card; left: thank-you cards and mailing label.

116

Poetry Reading, Sept. 23, Butler Square.

Mothers,

there's a mad man

running in the

streets,

And he's

humming a tune,

And he's

snarling at dogs,

And he still

has

four

more

miles

to go.

Just do it.

5:30 free beer, 7:00 dinner, 8:00 Jerry Cronin. Members free, non-members $20, students $10. Please rsvp to 220-4817 by September 20th.

Art Directors/Copywriters Club

AGENCY:

Clarity Coverdale Fury

Advertising, Inc.,

Minneapolis, Minnesota

ART DIRECTORS:

Randy Hughes,

David Jenkins

PHOTOGRAPHER:

Arthur Meyerson

COPYWRITERS:

Bill Johnson, Jerry Cronin

PURPOSE: To promote a

speaking engagement by

Jerry Cronin.

ART DIRECTOR/

DESIGNER/ILLUSTRATOR:

McRay Magleby,

University Publications,

Provo, Utah

SILKSCREENER:

Rory Robinson

PURPOSE: Promotional

Brigham Young University

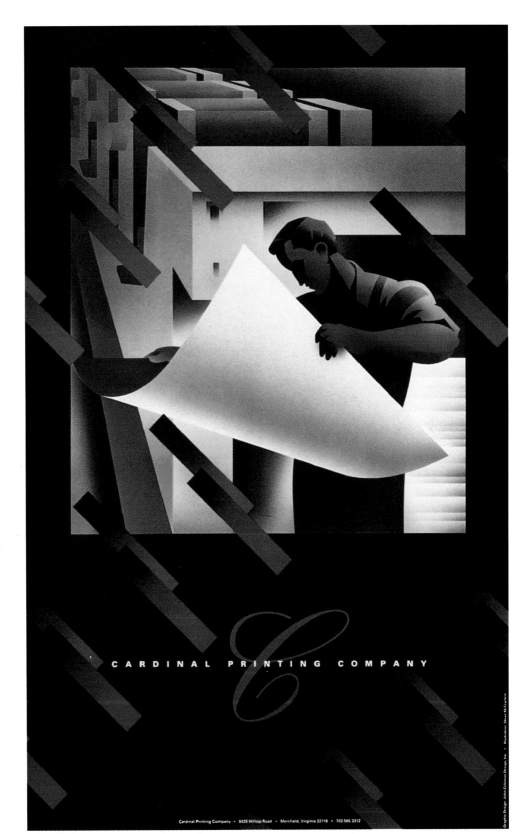

DESIGN FIRM:

John Coleman Design,

Washington, DC

ART DIRECTOR/

DESIGNER: John Coleman

ILLUSTRATOR:

Steve McCracken

PURPOSE: Promotional

Cardinal Printing

DESIGN FIRM:

Pannell St. George,

Dallas, Texas

ART DIRECTOR/

DESIGNER/ILLUSTRATOR:

Cap Pannell

COPYWRITER:

Carol St. George

BUDGET: $2500 for series

of three (printing only)

QUANTITY: 100-120

PRINTING PROCESS:

Silkscreen

PURPOSE: For display in

store to educate

customers about bakery's

commitment to quality,

service, and fresh bagels.

DESIGN FIRM: Mullen, Wenham, Massachusetts

CREATIVE DIRECTORS: Amy Watt, Edward Boches (Buttons, Turtles)

ART DIRECTORS: Amy Watt (Turtles, Triangle), Brenda Dziadzio (Turtles, Buttons)

DESIGNER: Jodi Wiedenroth (Triangle)

PHOTOGRAPHER: John Holt

COPYWRITERS: Roger Baldacci (Turtles, Buttons), Edward Boches (Triangle, Turtles)

PRINTING PROCESS: Sheet fed, 4-color

PURPOSE: Promotional

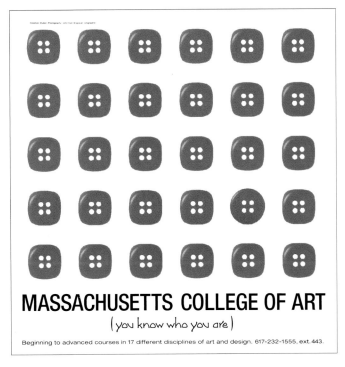

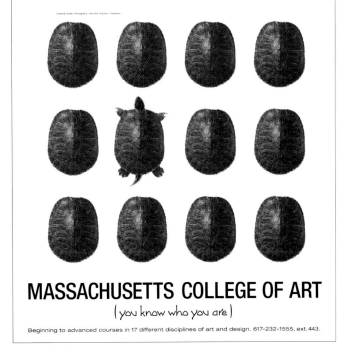

DESIGN FIRM: NBBJ Graphic Design, Seattle, Washington
ART DIRECTOR/DESIGNER: Klindt Parker
BUDGET: Designers solicited donations from vendors and the poster was designed in accordance with the donations they were able to secure.
QUANTITY: 500+
PRINTING PROCESS: 3-color silkscreen
PURPOSE: To promote a theatrical production.

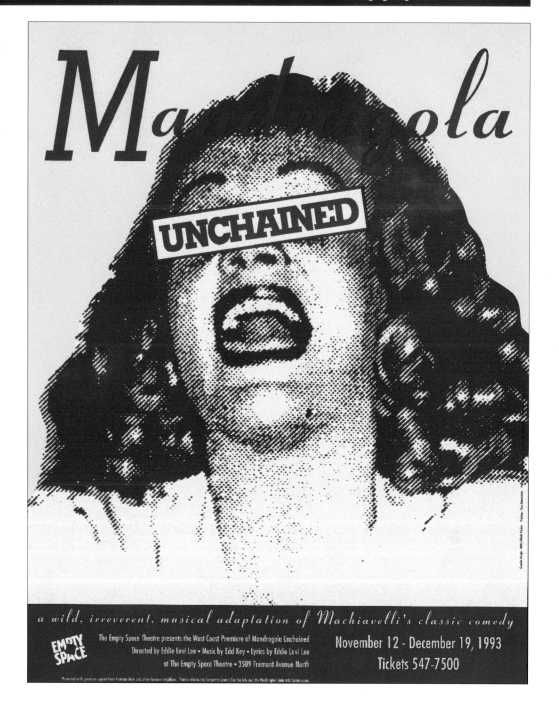

DESIGN FIRM:

Boram Design,

Seattle, Washington

ART DIRECTOR/

DESIGNER: Brian Boram

PHOTOGRAPHER:

Marion Gray

BUDGET: $1000

QUANTITY: 30,000

PRINTING PROCESS: Web

PURPOSE: To announce

and promote a theatrical

production.

DESIGN FIRM:

Modern Dog,

Seattle, Washington

ART DIRECTOR:

Vittorio Costarella,

Robynne Raye,

Michael Strassburger

DESIGNER/ILLUSTRATOR:

Vittorio Costarella

BUDGET: $2400 for

screenprinting, diecuts

QUANTITY: 700

PRINTING PROCESS:

Screenprint

PURPOSE: To promote a

theatrical production.

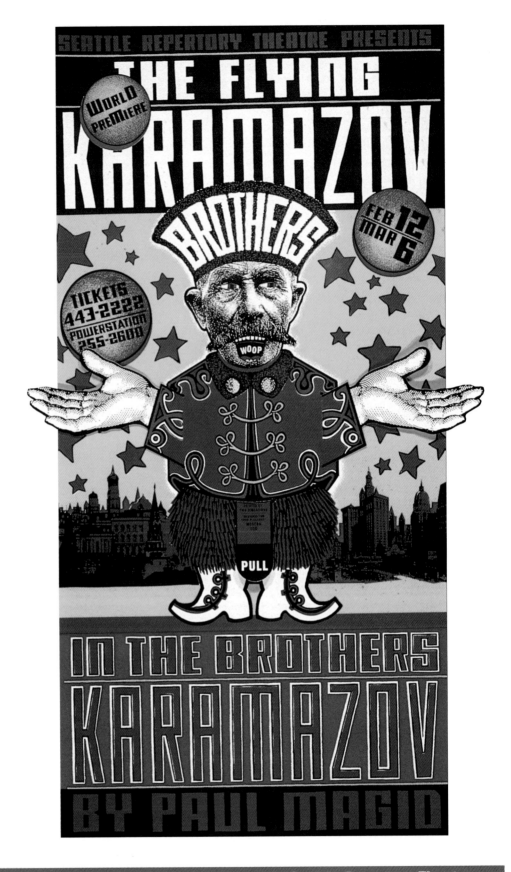

Seattle Repertory Theatre

DESIGN FIRM:

Paradigm:design,

Philadelphia, Pennsylvania

ART DIRECTOR/

DESIGNER: Joel Katz

ILLUSTRATOR:

Steven Lyons

PRINTING PROCESS:

Sheet-fed offset

PURPOSE: Promotional

*Below: cover of accompanying
promotional book.*

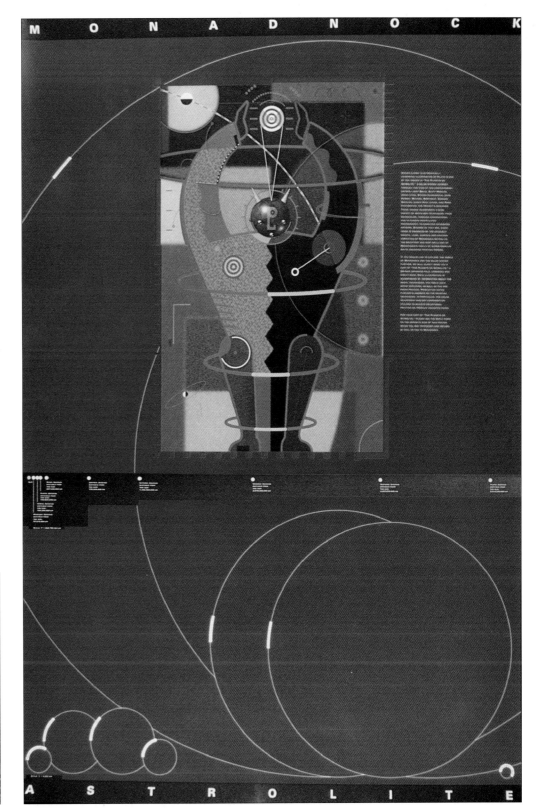

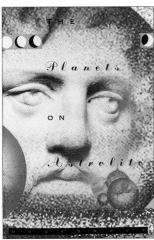

Monadnock Paper Mills, Inc.

Saul Mandel
ARTIST AND DESIGNER

STAMPS DESIGNED FOR THE UNITED NATIONS POSTAL ADMINISTRATION

ART DIRECTORS:

Saul Mandel, Cranbury,

New Jersey, Rocco Callari/

United Nations

DESIGNER/ILLUSTRATOR:

Saul Mandel

PURPOSE: To promote the

United Nations Postal

Administration and the

artist.

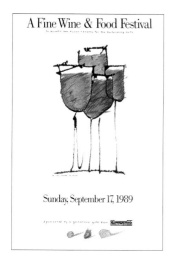

Above: poster for the 1989 event; top: hand-done opening night program.

Annual fine wine and food festival fundraiser.

DESIGN FIRM:

KAISERDICKEN, Burlington, Vermont

ART DIRECTOR:

Debra Kaiser

DESIGNER/ILLUSTRATOR:

Craig Dicken

SEPARATOR:

H. Horsman & Co.

PRINTER:

Queen City Printers

BUDGET: Pro bono (design, separations), at cost (printing)

QUANTITY: 500

PRINTING PROCESS:

4-color

PURPOSE: To announce and promote the event; also sold at the event.

DESIGN FIRM: TW Design, Decatur, Georgia

ART DIRECTOR: Andi Counts

ILLUSTRATOR: Bill Mayer

PURPOSE: In-house promotion for multimedia department. Poster was adapted from the cover of the company's in-house magazine, Multimedia Solutions. This issue focused on multimedia and museum exhibitions.

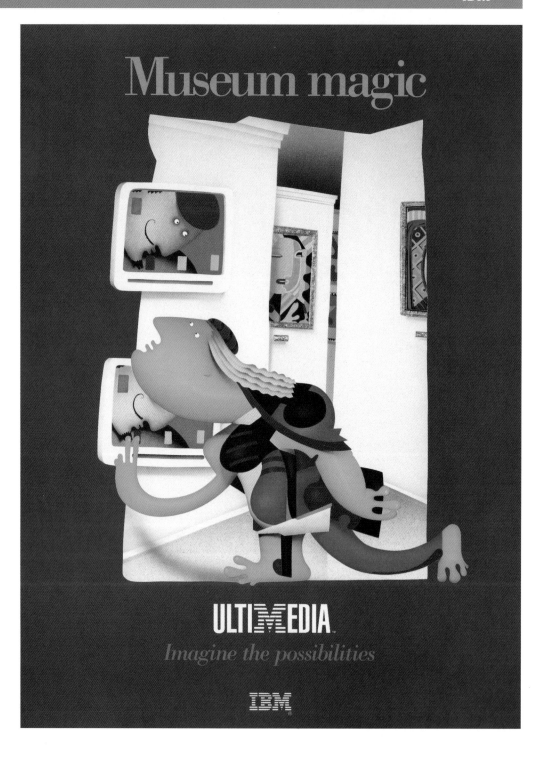

DESIGN FIRM:

Shepard Quraeshi
Associates, Chestnut Hill,
Massachusetts

ART DIRECTOR:

Samina Quraeshi

DESIGNER:

Tania Liepmann (poster);
Bryce Ambo (application);
Irene Chu, Tania Liepmann
(viewbook)

ILLUSTRATOR:

Robert Brinkerhoff

BUDGET: $30,000
(application, viewbook)

QUANTITY: 10,000

PRINTING PROCESS:

Offset lithography

PURPOSE: To inform high
schools when an M.I.T.
admissions representative
will be there to meet with
prospective applicants. Also
used as promotion for
M.I.T.

Far left: application; left: viewbook.

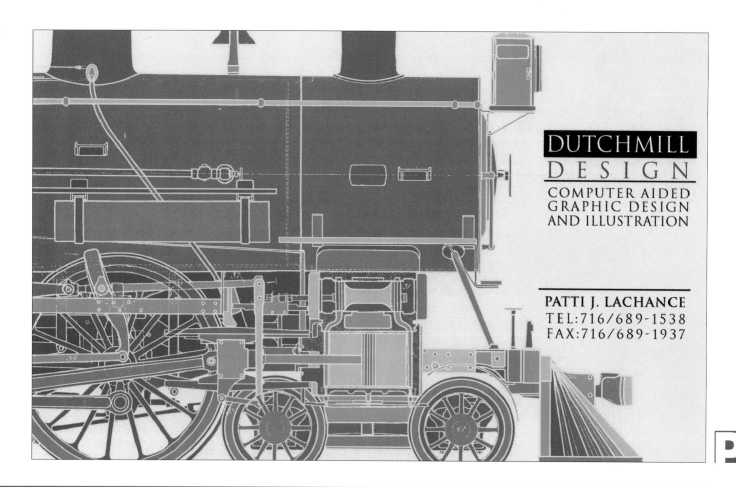

DESIGN FIRM:

Dutchmill Design,

Fairport, New York

ART DIRECTOR/

DESIGNER/ILLUSTRATOR:

Patti Lachance

BUDGET: $1150

QUANTITY: 50

PRINTING PROCESS:

Canon Fiery color output

PURPOSE: Self-promotion

targeting design studios

and agencies.

CINCUENTA ANIVERSARIO

DESIGN FIRM:

The Hill Group,

Houston, Texas

ART DIRECTOR: Chris Hill

DESIGNERS: Jeff Davis,

Tom Berno, Laura Menegaz

ILLUSTRATOR: Linda Bleck

PURPOSE:

To commemorate the

school's 50th anniversary.

Monterrey Tech University

Heart Broken?

 Cardiopulmonary Institute At King's Daughters.

We Have Some Of The Best Doctors In Circulation.

Cardiopulmonary Institute At King's Daughters.

AGENCY:	ART DIRECTOR:	PRINTING PROCESS:	broadcast) to let
Wolf Blumberg Krody, Inc.,	Scott Morris	4-color silkscreen	northwestern Kentucky
Cincinnati, Ohio	COPYWRITER: Mike Allen	PURPOSE: Billboard	residents know that they
CREATIVE DIRECTOR:	BUDGET: $18,000	segment of multimedia	can now obtain state-of-
Vern Hughes	QUANTITY: 14 billboards	campaign (outdoor, print,	the-art cardiopulmonary
			care close to home.

132

Fashion Institute of Technology

ART DIRECTOR:

Daisy Rosner/F.I.T.,

New York, New York

DESIGNER: Joerg Braeuer

ILLUSTRATOR:

Mari Lou Smith

PURPOSE: Invitation to

student art and design

exhibition.

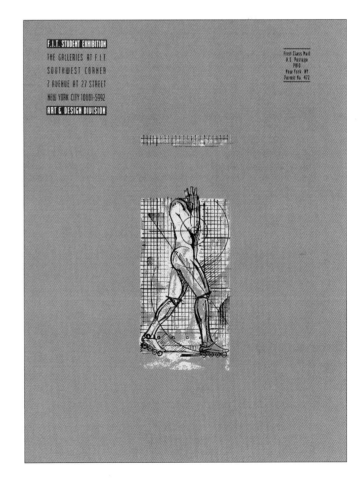

Poster folded as mailer.

DESIGN FIRM: Brainworks,

San Francisco, California

ART DIRECTOR/

DESIGNER: Al Kahn

PHOTOGRAPHER:

Nick Koudis

PURPOSE: National poster

campaign to prevent birth

defects from smoking and

drug and alcohol abuse.

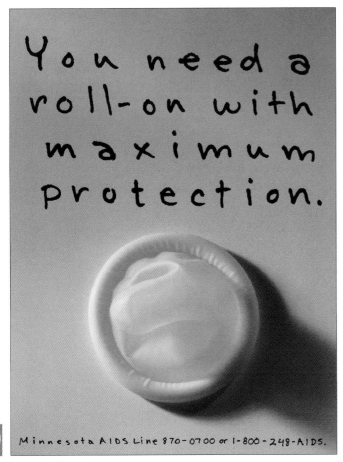

You need a
roll-on with
maximum
protection.

Minnesota AIDS Line 870-0700 or 1-800-248-AIDS.

When you give
the gift of love,
make sure it's
wrapped properly.

Minnesota AIDS Line 870-0700 or 1-800-248-AIDS.

Minnesota AIDS Line

Hot-line to answer

questions concerning

AIDS and its prevention

AGENCY: Martin/Williams,

Minneapolis, Minnesota

ART DIRECTOR:

Wayne Thompson

COPYWRITER: Tom Kelly

PURPOSE: To increase

public awareness of the

service.

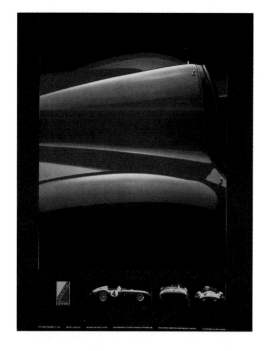

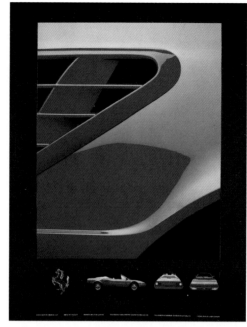

DESIGN FIRM: Graphtec,

Fort Lauderdale, Florida

ART DIRECTOR/

DESIGNER: Peter Jacaty

PHOTOGRAPHER:

Peter Langone

SEPARATOR/PRINTER:

Graphtec

VINTAGE FERRARIS

COURTESY: Larry Clemons

BUDGET: $120,000

QUANTITY: 3000 each,

12,000 total

PRINTING PROCESS:

4-color plus gloss/dull

varnish, plus two touch

plates, plus foil stamp, plus

embossing; 92# Trophy Dull

Cover

PURPOSE: Self-promotion

for Graphtec, Peter Jacaty

and Langone Studio.

Graphtec (Color Separations/Electronic Imaging/Sheet-fed Printing)

DESIGN FIRM:

Margie Adkins Graphic

Design, Fort Worth, Texas

ART DIRECTOR/

DESIGNER: Margie Adkins

PHOTOGRAPHER:

Arthur Meyerson

PRODUCTION:

Cockrell Printing

SEPARATOR: Barron Litho

QUANTITY: 1000

PRINTING PROCESS:

Offset

PURPOSE: Promotion for

photographer and printer.

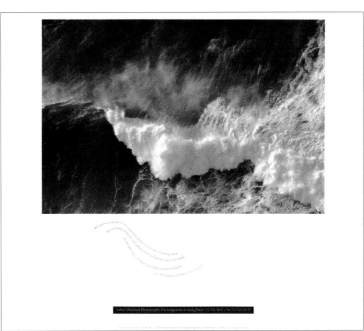

The University Of Minnesota Hosts

The 1993 NCAA Division I Women's Swimming And Diving Championships.

March 18-20. University Aquatic Center. For ticket information, please call 624-8080.

AGENCY: Martin/Williams, Minneapolis, Minnesota

ART DIRECTOR: Jeff Jahn

PHOTOGRAPHER: Shawn Michienzi

COPYWRITER: Lyle Wedemeyer

QUANTITY: 10,000

PRINTING PROCESS: 4-color lithography

PURPOSE: To announce that the University of Minnesota would host the 1993 NCAA Division I Women's Swimming and Diving Championships.

DESIGN FIRM:

Mires Design,

San Diego, California

ART DIRECTOR:

José Serrano

DESIGNERS: José Serrano,

Mike Brower

ILLUSTRATOR:

Tracy Sabin (1992),

Gerald Bustamante (1993)

PRINTER:

Gordon Screen Printing

BUDGET: $1000 (1992)

QUANTITY: 1000 (1992),

2000 (1993)

PRINTING PROCESS:

Silkscreen (1992),

4-color (1993)

PURPOSE: To announce

the 8th and 9th annual

Rowing and Paddling

Regattas.

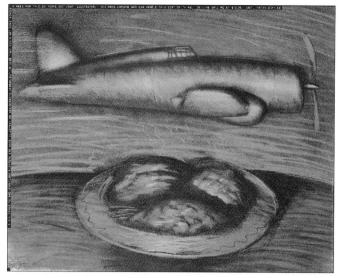

Regan Dunnick (Illustrator)

DESIGN FIRM:

The Hill Group,

Houston, Texas

ART DIRECTOR: Chris Hill

DESIGNERS: Jeff Davis,

Chris Hill

ILLUSTRATOR:

Regan Dunnick

TYPOGRAPHER:

Dyno Hobbyist

PRINTING PROCESS:

4-color offset

PURPOSE: Self-promotion

Shelter for runaway and troubled youths.

DESIGN FIRM:

Sayles Graphic Design, Des Moines, Iowa

CREATIVE DIRECTOR:

Wendy Lyons

DESIGNER: John Sayles

BUDGET: Pro bono

QUANTITY: 250

PRINTING PROCESS:

Screenprinted on emerald green (Gilbert Oxford) uncoated paper, using flat poster inks to produce a chalky effect reminiscent of 1930s advertising.

PURPOSE: To promote fundraising event soliciting hotel amenities (trial-size shampoo, toothpaste, etc.) so the shelter wouldn't have to spend operating capital on these items. The event collected enough to last a full year.

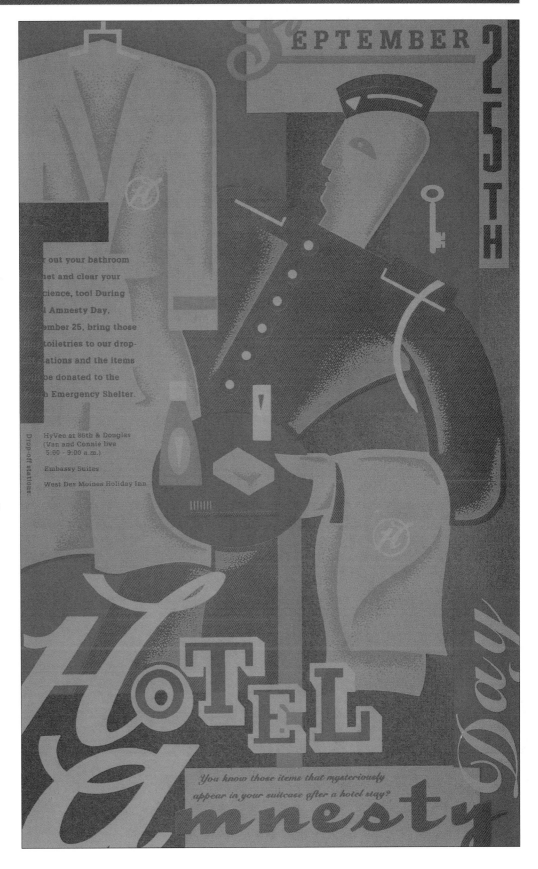

ART DIRECTOR/

DESIGNER: Art Chantry,

Seattle, Washington

PRINTER: Art Garcia

BUDGET: Pro bono

QUANTITY:

150 (silkscreen)

5000 (newsprint)

PRINTING PROCESS:

Silkscreen (limited

edition), web newspaper

offset (newsprint)

PURPOSE: To promote a

show of hot-rod artists.

The newsprint version

was for a general mailing;

the silkscreen edition was

sold to raise funds to cover

expenses.

DESIGN FIRM: Graffito,

Baltimore, Maryland

ART DIRECTOR:

Tim Thompson

DESIGNER/ILLUSTRATOR:

Dave Plunkert

BUDGET: $17,500

QUANTITY: 5000

PRINTING PROCESS:

5 colors (process plus

1 PMS)

PURPOSE: To promote

Intelsat's role in

broadcasting the 1992

Barcelona Olympics

worldwide via satellite.

Racism and the Death Penalty

DESIGN FIRM:

Victore Design Works,

New York, New York

ART DIRECTOR:

James Victore

WRITER: Kica Matos

BUDGET: $2500

QUANTITY: 5000

PRINTING PROCESS:

Offset

PURPOSE: To advertise a

documentary film and

serve on its own as an

educational tool.

NAACP/ACLU Legal Defense Fund

SHAKESPEARE SERIES, PAVILION THEATRE, JUNE 4 & 5, 8 PM.

DESIGN FIRM:

Sommese Design, State

College, Pennsylvania

ART DIRECTOR/

DESIGNER/ILLUSTRATOR:

Lanny Sommese

BUDGET: $150

QUANTITY: 75

PRINTING PROCESS:

Silkscreen

PURPOSE: To announce a

theatrical production.

Penn State Theater Department Summer Series

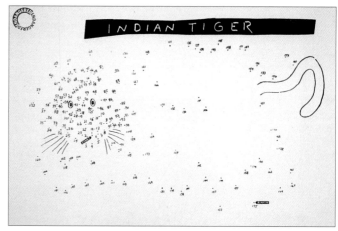

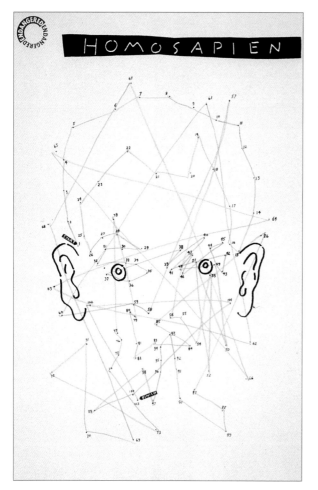

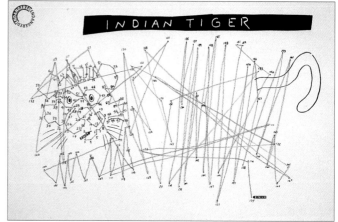

DESIGN FIRM:

Sommese Design, State

College, Pennsylvania

ART DIRECTOR/

DESIGNER/ILLUSTRATOR:

Lanny Sommese

PRINTER: Jim Lilly

BUDGET: $200

QUANTITY: 100

PRINTING PROCESS:

Silkscreen

PURPOSE: A series of

posters designed as a grant

project to call attention to

various endangered

subjects: some animals, but

also other things such as

fashions and morals.

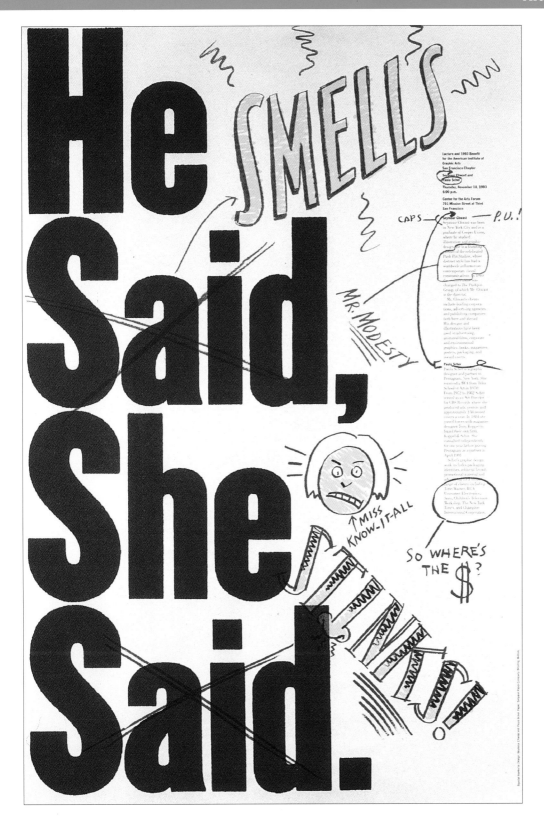

DESIGN FIRM:

Pentagram Design,

New York, New York

ART DIRECTORS/

DESIGNERS/

ILLUSTRATORS:

Paula Scher,

Seymour Chwast

PRINTER: Mobius

PAPER: Simpson Paper

Company

PURPOSE: To promote a

speaking engagement by

Scher and Chwast.

DESIGN FIRM:

The Hill Group,

Houston, Texas

ART DIRECTOR: Jeff Davis

DESIGNERS: Jeff Davis,

Tom Berno

PHOTOGRAPHER:

Mark Green

COPYWRITER: Tom Berno

PRINTING PROCESS:

4-color offset

PURPOSE: Invitation to a

lecture by D.J. Stout, art

director of Texas Monthly.

The Art Director's Club of Houston is serving up a special event at Houston's noted design pub, Innova, on Thursday, March 17. And it won't feature just any pint-sized talent. We've imported the award-winning art director of *Texas Monthly*: D.J. Stout. He will reveal his own special blend of sophisticated layout and Texas humor that has resulted in a design tradition that's always rich and full-bodied, never watered-down. And if that isn't enough Stout for you, Grif's Irish Pub will cater a cash bar to serve all of the proper holiday spirits, courtesy of Haywood Graphics. We'll even have a bagpipe player at the social hour, which begins at 6:00 p.m. Program starts at 7:00. So join us at Innova and kick off your St. Patrick's Day celebration with D.J. Stout. And tap into one of the premium designers working today. Admission is $8 for ADCH members and students with ID, and $12 for non-members.

AGENCY:

Bernstein-Rein Advertising,

Kansas City, Missouri

CREATIVE DIRECTOR:

Tim Hamill

ART DIRECTOR:

Eric Baumgartner

PHOTOGRAPHER:

David Ludwigs

COPYWRITER:

Jeff Bremser

PURPOSE: To promote

Vintage Kansas City wine-

tasting fundraiser.

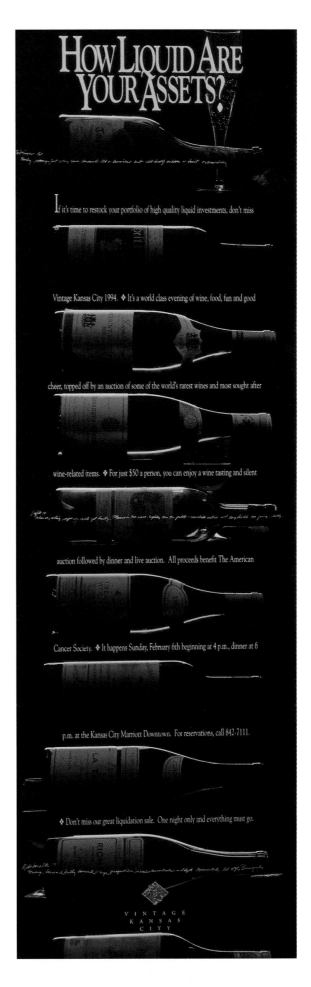

ART DIRECTOR:

Scott Wadler/

MTV Networks,

New York, New York

DESIGNER: Karl Cantarella

BUDGET: $300 for design

QUANTITY: 6

PRINTING PROCESS:

4-color

PURPOSE: Station I.D. for

The End 107.7.

AGENCY: Mullen,

Wenham, Massachusetts

ART DIRECTOR:

Brenda Dziadzio

COPYWRITER:

Paul Silverman

PURPOSE: Promotional

DESIGN FIRM:

Fotofolio, Inc.,

New York, New York

ART DIRECTOR/

DESIGNER: Ron Schick

PHOTOGRAPHER:

William Wegman

QUANTITY: 1000

PRINTING PROCESS:

Offset

PURPOSE: To publicize

the 30th New York Film

Festival.

THE HAZARDS OF BEING A CHAIR

CONFLICT

RULES & REGULATIONS

STRESS

BUDGET CUTS

FAILURE

BURN OUT

The National Community College Chair Academy Announces The Second Annual Conference of Community College Chairs
Phoenix, Arizona   February 17-20, 1993

ACADEMY

DESIGN FIRM: After Hours, Phoenix, Arizona

ART DIRECTOR: Russ Haan

DESIGNER: Brad Smith

ILLUSTRATOR: Carolyn Fisher (mailer)

PHOTOGRAPHER: Art Holeman (poster)

BUDGET: $5000-$6000 (poster), $7000 (mailer)

QUANTITY: 12,000 (poster), 13,000 (mailer)

PRINTING PROCESS: Offset lithography

PURPOSE: To announce the 1993 conference of the National Association of Department Chairs.

Above: promotional mailer; below, left: logo from promotional booklet; below, right: promotional T-shirt.

The NIH Public Affairs Forum presents an Open House of the

MEDICAL ARTS & PHOTOGRAPHY BRANCH

January 26, 1993, 1-4 p.m.

Building 10, B2 Level

Five concurrent demonstrations:

Computer-Aided Graphic Design

Converting Data to Charts, Graphs, & Slides

Exhibits on the Go

The Latest in Video and Medical Illustration

Multi-Media Slide Show

For more information call Bill Hall

496-1144

ART DIRECTORS:

Ron Winterrowd,

Linda Brown/National

Institutes of Health,

Bethesda, Maryland

DESIGNER: Karen Connery

BUDGET: Pro bono

QUANTITY: 100-200

PRINTING PROCESS:

Silkscreen

PURPOSE: To announce an

open house at the Medical

Arts & Photography Branch

for communications

specialists, designers and

the NIH community.

DESIGN FIRM:
Young & Laramore,
Indianapolis, Indiana
CREATIVE DIRECTORS:
David Young, Jeff Laramore
ART DIRECTOR/
DESIGNER: Carolyn Hadlock
ILLUSTRATOR: James Yang
WRITER: Charlie Hopper
QUANTITY: 1500
PRINTING PROCESS:
4-color plus two PMS colors
and varnish, reversed type
out of 4-color
PURPOSE: Part of poster
series advertising Kubin-
Nicholson's large printing
press—sent as a sample to
clients.

STRATHMORE

RECOGNIZING IMAGINATION &

GRAPHICS

THE POWER OF THE PRINTED IMAGE

GALLERY

IN GRAPHIC COMMUNICATIONS

DESIGN FIRM:

Pollard Design,

East Hartland, Connecticut

AGENCY/PROJECT

COORDINATION:

Williams & House

DESIGNERS: Jeff Pollard,

Adrienne Pollard

ILLUSTRATOR:

Anthony Russo

PRINTING PROCESS:

Offset lithography

PURPOSE: Call-for-entries

Top: entry forms; center: award; bottom: promotional blank notebook.

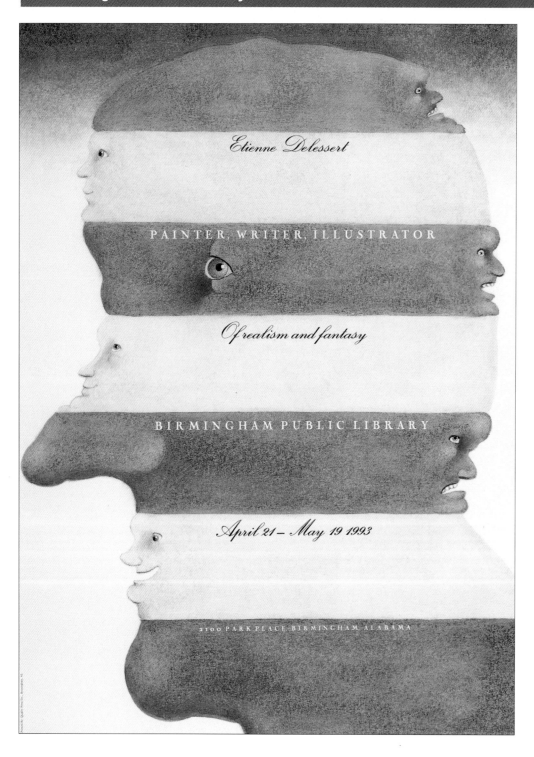

DESIGN FIRM:

Delessert & Marshall,

Lakeville, Connecticut

ART DIRECTOR/

DESIGNER: Rita Marshall

ILLUSTRATOR:

Etienne Delessert

QUANTITY: 1000 per city

PRINTING PROCESS:

4-color offset

PURPOSE: To advertise a

traveling retrospective

exhibition in six American

cities.

Annual summer celebration of the visual and performing arts.

DESIGN FIRM:

Sommese Design, State College, Pennsylvania

ART DIRECTOR/ DESIGNER:

Lanny Sommese

BUDGET: $3500 (excluding design)

QUANTITY: 1000

PRINTING PROCESS:

Offset

PURPOSE: Promotional; also sold as a collectible.

Below: call-for-entries brochures.

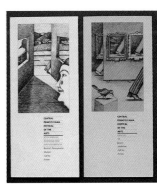

DESIGN FIRM:

Pentagram Design,

New York, New York

ART DIRECTOR:

Paula Scher

DESIGNERS: Paula Scher,

Ron Louie

PRINTER:

Ambassador Arts

PAPER: Champion Benefit

TYPOGRAPHY: Typogram

PURPOSE: To promote

inaugural conference and

exhibition at the Center.

Above: Identity applied to banners.

Richard & Marieluise Black Center for Curatorial Studies & Art in Contemporary Culture

POSSIBILITIES

NOT RACE. NOT CLASS. NOTHING CAN HOLD YOUR STUDENTS BACK
BUT IGNORANCE. PUT THE POWER IN THEIR HANDS.

MATH IS POWER

OPPORTUNITY EMPLOYER

FORGET EVERYTHING YOU'VE HEARD ABOUT QUOTAS.
KNOWLEDGE IS WHAT'LL GET YOU THE JOB. PUT THE POWER IN YOUR HANDS.

MATH IS POWER

National Action Council for Minorities in Engineering

AND CONQUER

IT'S TRUE, YOU CAN BE WHATEVER YOU WANT TO BE.
YOU JUST NEED TO LEARN HOW. PUT THE POWER IN YOUR HANDS.

MATH IS POWER

Non-profit organization that encourages minorities to study math as a path to becoming engineers ("Math is Power").

DESIGN FIRM: Tracy-Locke/DDB Needham, Dallas, Texas

ART DIRECTOR: Jonathan Rice

ILLUSTRATORS: Jonathan Rice, Louie Reynolds

COPYWRITER: Lynn Glickman

BUDGET: Pro bono

QUANTITY: 500

PRINTING PROCESS: Custom opaque based PMS inks; background color was double bumped, printed on 6-color 40-inch Akiyama press.

PURPOSE: To encourage minority students to enroll in math classes.

BALANCE / PROFORX BY ANSWER
DESIGNED AND MANUFACTURED

NEUTRAL PIVOT POSITION ALLOWS FOR

FULLY ACTIVE
SUSPENSION

[ADJUSTABLE SPRING ELASTOMER
WITH 2.8" REAR WHEEL TRAVEL]

ZERO BIOPACE EFFECT
...ZERO PEDAL STROKE WAS...

E TICKET

WORLD DOWNHILL CHAMPIONSHIP
1993

IN 1993 BALANCE CYCLES COMPETED IN THEIR FIRST FULL SEASON OF PRO RACING. AFTER THE DUST HAD SETTLED, BALANCE EMERGED WITH A [NORBA] NATIONAL DUAL SLALOM CHAMPIONSHIP AS WELL AS THE WORLD DOWNHILL CHAMPIONSHIP. BALANCE CYCLES IS NOW PREPARING IT'S 1994 ATTACK AND LOOKING FOR RIDERS. IF YOU'RE INTERESTED IN BECOMING A BALANCE CO-FACTORY RIDER CONTACT YOUR LOCAL BALANCE DEALER FOR DETAILS.

FORK OPTIONS
ANSWER MANITOU III
PROFORX ST
(WORLD DOWNHILL CHAMPION FORK)
PROFORX LT

USA ASSEMBLED
R.I.D.
RIDER INTEGRATED DESIGN

FULL SUSPENSION FRAMESET
7005 SERIES
ALUMINUM
STRAIGHT GAUGE
ALCOA TUBING

B BALANCE

RIDE: BALANCE FS.PRO TYPE: FULL SUSPENSION FRAMESET FRAME: 7005 SERIES ALUMINUM, STRAIGHT GAUGE ALCOA TUBING COLOR: EMERALD MIRROR FADE. REAR SUSPENSION: PRO FORX ADJUSTABLE SPRING ELASTOMER, 2.8" REAR WHEEL TRAVEL (3.8" ALSO AVAILABLE) PIVOT: NEEDLE BEARING, ZIRK GREASE FITTING FRONT SUSPENSION (OPTION): ANSWER MANITOU III OR MANITOU SPORT, PROFORX ST OR LT HEADSET: DIA COMPE AHEADSET FOR MORE INFO: 800.727.1922

ART DIRECTOR:

Sergio Bravo/

Smith, Smith & Smith,

Redondo, California

PHOTOGRAPHER:

Sean Thonson

BUDGET: $4300

(printing only)

QUANTITY: 5000

PRINTING PROCESS:

5-color plus varnish;

separations from a

composed desktop file

PURPOSE: To help promote

introduction of Balance's

new full-suspension bike.

Balance Cycles (Mountain Bikes)

DESIGN FIRM:

Johnson Design,

Sonoma, California

ART DIRECTOR/

DESIGNER/ILLUSTRATOR:

Bob Johnson

PRINTER: Paragraphics

QUANTITY: 3000

PRINTING PROCESS:

Offset

PURPOSE: To promote

Bob Johnson art show and

the winery.

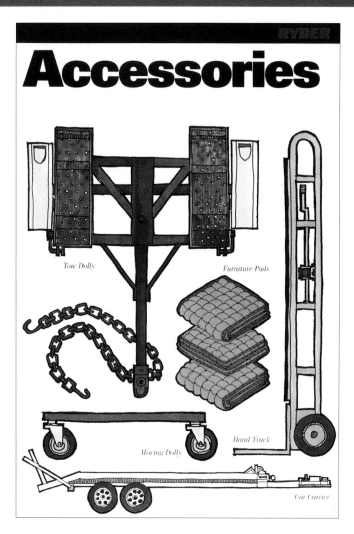

Accessories

RYDER

Tow Dolly

Furniture Pads

Hand Truck

Moving Dolly

Car Carrier

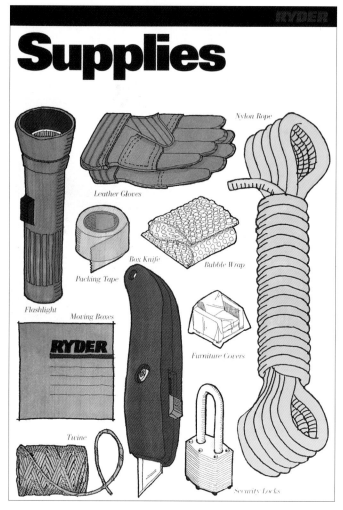

Supplies

RYDER

Nylon Rope

Leather Gloves

Box Knife

Bubble Wrap

Packing Tape

Flashlight

Moving Boxes

RYDER

Furniture Covers

Twine

Security Locks

DESIGN FIRM:

Powell + Associates,

Newnan, Georgia

ART DIRECTOR/

ILLUSTRATOR:

Doug Powell

DESIGNERS: Eric Etheridge,

Dave Bevacqua

QUANTITY: 10,000

PRINTING PROCESS:

Offset

PURPOSE: Point-of-

purchase promotion.

Moving Vans

RYDER

RYDER

RYDER

RYDER

RYDER

An international
student think tank.
DESIGN FIRM:
Crocker, Inc.,
Brookline, Massachusetts
ART DIRECTOR/
DESIGNER/ILLUSTRATOR:
Bruce Crocker
PRODUCTION:
Fine Arts Press
PRINTING PROCESS:
Silkscreen
PURPOSE: To promote a
special project of the
Creative Education
Foundation.

DESIGN FIRM:

A Houston Advertising,

Atlanta, Georgia

ART DIRECTOR:

Ann Houston

COPYWRITER: Cathy Adler

BUDGET: $2500

(creative only)

QUANTITY: 1

PURPOSE: Promotional

DESIGN FIRM: Royal Design,

Memphis, Tennessee

ART DIRECTOR/

DESIGNER/ILLUSTRATOR:

Royal Design

PRINTER: Serigraphics

QUANTITY: 500

PRINTING PROCESS: Hand

silkscreened (3-color) on

French Cortone

PURPOSE: To announce the

establishment of the firm

and promote it to agencies

and prospective clients.

The tractor that pulled the
competition into the 90's.

*Above and below: ads from the
same campaign.*

Remember
when you
first decided
to farm?

AGENCY:

Gouchenour Advertising,

Orlando, Florida

ART DIRECTORS/

DESIGNERS:

Lynn Hawkins, Chris Robb

PHOTOGRAPHER:

Joe Baraban

COPYWRITER: Bob Gotron

QUANTITY: 1000

PRINTING PROCESS:

4-color

PURPOSE: Dealer point-of-

purchase.

AGCO Allis tractors.
Currently making waves at your local dealer.

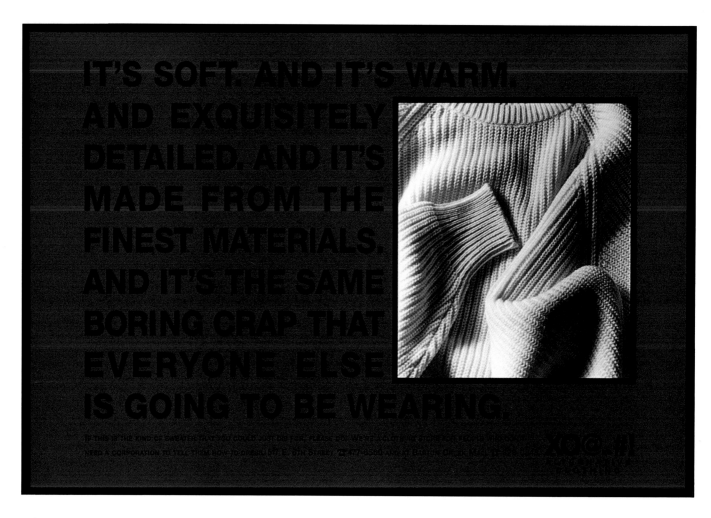

IT'S SOFT. AND IT'S WARM. AND EXQUISITELY DETAILED. AND IT'S MADE FROM THE FINEST MATERIALS. AND IT'S THE SAME BORING CRAP THAT EVERYONE ELSE IS GOING TO BE WEARING.

AGENCY:

GSD&M Advertising,

Austin, Texas

ART DIRECTOR:

Mike Bevil

PHOTOGRAPHER:

Richard Reens

COPYWRITER: Tim Bauer

BUDGET: Under $5000

QUANTITY: 5000 each of

three posters

PRINTING PROCESS:

4-color

PURPOSE: Point-of-

purchase promotion.

YOU CAN BUY A DANCE AND YOU CAN BUY A JUDGE. YOU CAN BUY A WOMAN AND YOU CAN BUY A VOWEL. YOU CAN BUY NEW CHEEKBONES. YOU CAN BUY PUBLICITY, AN ALIBI, A STAR AND A PARDON. YOU CAN BUY SOMEONE'S LOYALTY. YOU CAN BUY ANOTHER'S AFFECTION. YOU CAN BUY YOUR WAY OUT. EVERYTHING, EVERYTHING IS FOR SALE. YOU CAN GO TO THE EIGHTEENTH SEATTLE INTERNATIONAL FILM FESTIVAL. BUT ONLY IF YOU BUY TICKETS.

GO TO THE BROADWAY MARKET OR CALL 325.2485

AGENCY: Cole & Weber, Seattle, Washington

ART DIRECTOR:

Steve Luker

COPYWRITER:

Steven Johnston

PRODUCTION MANAGER:

Wanda Nichols

BUDGET: $100

QUANTITY: 100

PRINTING PROCESS:

Offset

PURPOSE: To encourage people to buy advance tickets to the festival.

Seattle International Film Festival

JUST DUNE IT

ART DIRECTOR/

DESIGNER:

Madeleine Fishman,

Corte Madera, California

PHOTOGRAPHER:

Gary Brettnacher

BUDGET: $893

QUANTITY: 5000

PRINTING PROCESS:

Offset lithography

PURPOSE: For retail sale.

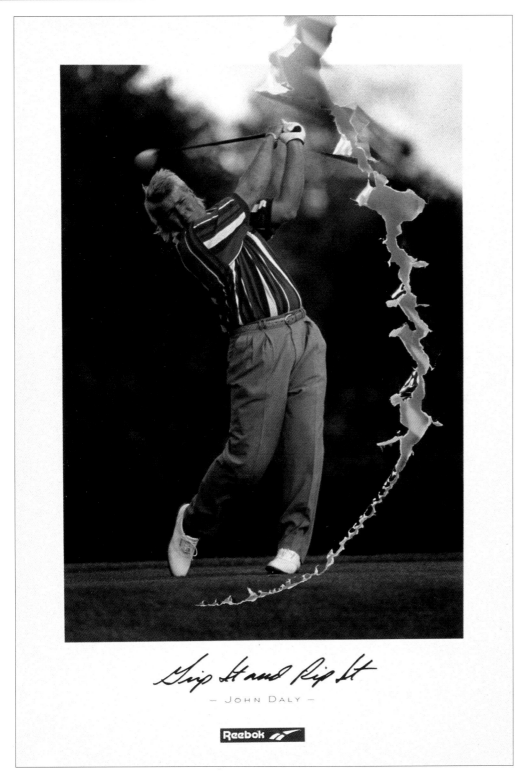

Grip It and Rip It

— JOHN DALY —

Reebok

AGENCY: Mullen, Wenham, Massachusetts

CREATIVE DIRECTOR: Edward Boches

ART DIRECTOR: Karen Lynch

DESIGNER: Dan Casey

PHOTOGRAPHERS: J. Rick Martin, Jack Richmond

COPYWRITER: Edward Boches

SEPARATOR: Unigraphic

BUDGET: $20,000

QUANTITY: 10,000

PRINTING PROCESS: Web, 4-color

PURPOSE: Promotional

DropThe Bomb.

If that ticking under the hood ▌ is starting to get on your nerves, then maybe you should check out the Langley Federal Credit Union Car Sale and our great rates on car loans. Because you never know when that ticking may stop.

The Langley Federal Credit Union Car Loan. ◢

This offer applies to LFCU members only. For more information, call 827-LFCU. ©1992 LFCU

Credit union located in Hampton, Virginia, with a large membership of Air Force personnel.

DESIGN FIRM:
Raoust & Gearhart, Hampton, Virginia

CREATIVE DIRECTOR:
Olivier Raoust

ART DIRECTOR:
Alan Schutte

PHOTOGRAPHER:
Craig Brewer

COPYWRITER:
Tom Campion

BUDGET: $4000

QUANTITY: 50

PRINTING PROCESS:
2-color silkscreen

PURPOSE: Point-of-purchase poster to promote automobile loans through a joint credit union/dealer program.

Pass.

Fail.

See what happens when you fall asleep in class? 861-1337.

BART'S SUBURBAN DRIVING SCHOOL

Meet our Principal.

He's big. He's mean. And he likes to hide behind things and tag you when you least expect it. 861-1337.

BART'S SUBURBAN DRIVING SCHOOL

You are here.

I'm over here with my foot planted firmly on the brake.

We don't want you to think we don't trust you, but the fact is, we don't. 861-1337.

Attend our school and get a really ugly graduation photo.

Hey, it's not our fault. Blame it on the lady at the DMV. 861-1337.

DESIGN FIRM:

Clarity Coverdale Fury

Advertising, Inc.,

Minneapolis, Minnesota

ART DIRECTOR:

Randy Hughes

PHOTOGRAPHY:

Curtis Johnson/Arndt

Photography

COPYWRITER:

Bill Johnson

PURPOSE: Promotional

Bart's Suburban Driving School

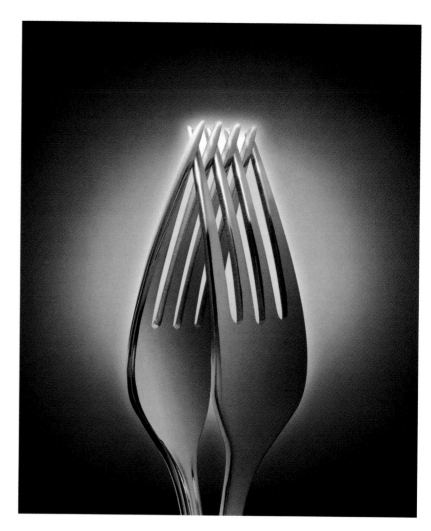

Before we eat, let's remember all we have to be thankful for.

Happy Thanksgiving.

Bozell
MINNEAPOLIS

AGENCY:

Bozell Worldwide/

Minneapolis, Minnesota

CREATIVE DIRECTOR:

Bert Gardner

ART DIRECTOR:

Anne Taylor

COPYWRITER:

Scott Jorgensen

PURPOSE: Self-promotion

Bozell Worldwide (Advertising)

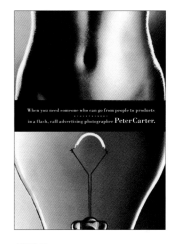

For a photographer whose skill with products is matched

4 1 4 • 4 7 6 • 6 0 0 1

only by his eye for fashion, just call **Peter Carter.**

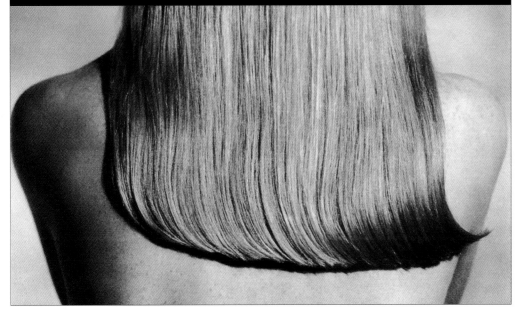

Peter Carter Photography

PHOTOGRAPHER:

Peter Carter,

Madison, Wisconsin

AGENCY:

All-Madden Group

ART DIRECTOR:

Scott Conklin

PURPOSE: Self-promotion

AGENCY:

Slaughter-Hanson,

Birmingham, Alabama

ART DIRECTOR/

DESIGNER: Marion English

PHOTOGRAPHER:

Lise Metzger

QUANTITY: 1500

PRINTING PROCESS:

Tri-tone, two blacks and

a PMS gray

PURPOSE: Self-promotion

DARKHORSE FILMS

Are you losing your husband to some skinny bitch?

For some people, compulsive gambling can become an obsession. It takes over lives, changes personalities, and ruins marriages. If someone you love needs help quitting, contact the Compulsive Gambling Hotline. **Minnesota Compulsive Gambling Hotline 1-800-437-3641**

You don't have to do drugs to get hooked by a dealer.

Compulsive gambling can be every bit as addictive as drugs. And every bit as destructive. It's not just cards, either. It's pull tabs. The lottery. And every other kind of gambling. If you need help quitting, call the Minnesota Compulsive Gambling Hotline. **Minnesota Compulsive Gambling Hotline 1-800-437-3641**

Just because you're sixteen doesn't mean you can't be up to your eyeballs in debt.

You may be a minor, but your gambling debts may not be. It's not hard for a teenager to run up hundreds of dollars in debts. The time to quit is before you get in too deep. For help, call the Minnesota Compulsive Gambling Hotline. Break the habit before the habit breaks you. **Minnesota Compulsive Gambling Hotline 1-800-437-3641**

AGENCY:

Clarity Coverdale Fury

Advertising, Inc.,

Minneapolis, Minnesota

ART DIRECTOR:

Jac Coverdale

PHOTOGRAPHER:

Steve Umland

COPYWRITER: Bill Johnson

PURPOSE: To promote a

hot-line.

Compulsive Gambling Hotline

DESIGN FIRM:

Chris Noel Design, Inc.,

Gaithersburg, Maryland

ART DIRECTOR/

DESIGNER: Chris Noel

ILLUSTRATOR:

John Howard

PURPOSE: Promotional

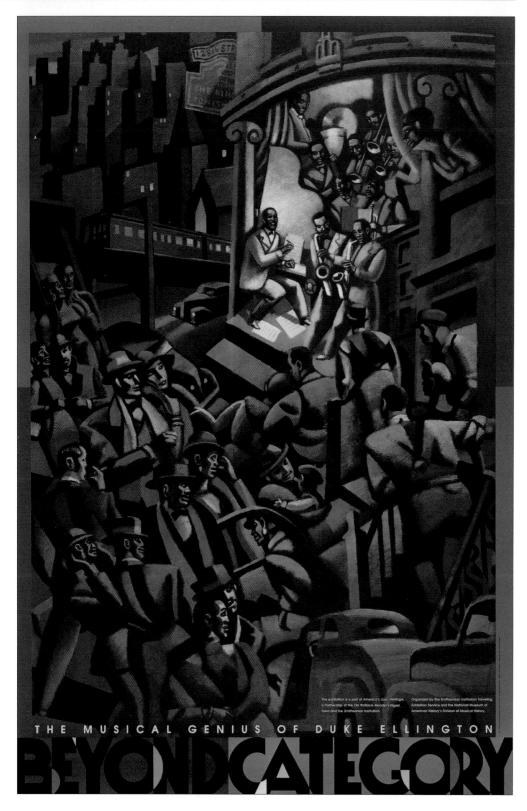

Below: cover of promotional folder.

IS ANYONE THERE?

Jennifer 8

IS NEXT

NOVEMBER 6

AGENCY: Concepts Arts, Hollywood, California

ART DIRECTORS: Lucinda Cowell, Ron Michaelson

DESIGNERS: Jen MaHarry, Evan Wright

PHOTOGRAPHER: Sheila Metzner

PURPOSE: Promotion for a film.

Apparently, Breakfast Cereal Isn't The Only Thing That Can Be Fortified With Iron.

If You Think Predicting The Stock Market Is Stressful, Try Predicting The Weather.

What Kind Of Shape Is The Future Of Our Country In?

Ironically, Many People Know More About Getting Shots For The One-Year-Old On The Left.

AGENCY:

Clarity Coverdale Fury

Advertising, Inc.,

Minneapolis, Minnesota

ART DIRECTOR:

Randy Hughes

COPYWRITER:

Jerry Fury

PURPOSE: Promotional

Organization promoting
gun control.

DESIGN FIRM:

Earle Palmer Brown/

Richmond, Virginia

ART DIRECTOR: Ty Harper

PHOTOGRAPHER:

Dean Hawthorne

COPYWRITER:

Rob Schapiro

PRODUCTION:

Robin Blanks

PURPOSE: Promotional

IT'S SO SIMPLE, EVEN A CHILD CAN DO IT.

Firing handguns may be simple. But passing laws to restrict them isn't. To find out how you can help call 1-800-4 DISARM.

COALITION TO STOP GUN VIOLENCE

Gun Coalition Against Violence

DESIGN FIRM:

Haley Johnson Design Co.,

Minneapolis, Minnesota

DESIGNER/ILLUSTRATOR:

Haley Johnson

QUANTITY: 500

PRINTING PROCESS:

Silkscreen

PURPOSE: Promotional

Boy Scouts of America, Viking Council

DESIGN FIRM:

Charles S. Anderson

Design Company,

Minneapolis, Minnesota

CREATIVE DIRECTOR:

Lisa Pemrick

ART DIRECTOR:

Charles S. Anderson

DESIGNERS:

Charles S. Anderson,

Todd Piper-Hauswirth

PURPOSE: To promote a

speaking engagement by

Anderson.

It May Not Be The Pearly Gates, But It's Pretty Close To Heaven.

It's Like A Whole Other Country

AGENCY:

GSD&M Advertising,

Austin, Texas

ART DIRECTOR:

Brent Ladd

PHOTOGRAPHER:

Dennis Murphy

COPYWRITER:

Brian Brooker

BUDGET: $4428

QUANTITY: 1000

PRINTING PROCESS:

4-color

PURPOSE: To promote

Texas tourism

Texas Department of Commerce

THESE WATERS SEPARATE OUR ISLANDS FROM
THE COAST. AND YOU FROM YOUR CARES.

When you're ready to put some distance between yourself and the workaday world, come to the barrier islands of North Carolina. A word of warning, though: you may find it hard to separate yourself from here when it's time to leave. NORTH CAROLINA

AGENCY:

Loeffler Ketchum Mountjoy,

Charlotte, North Carolina

ART DIRECTOR:

Tom Rouston

PHOTOGRAPHER:

Steve Murray

COPYWRITER:

Steve Skibba

PURPOSE: Promotional

North Carolina Travel and Tourism

Big Sky, Montana.

get in GEAR

LA GEAR

Below: other posters in series.

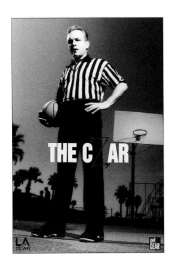

CREATIVE DIRECTOR:

Adam Bleibtreu/L.A. Gear,

Santa Monica, California

ART DIRECTOR:

Mark Hriciga, Keith Cooper

PHOTOGRAPHER:

Mark Hanauer

COPYWRITER:

Jennifer Joseph

PRINT PRODUCER:

Simon Barrett

PURPOSE: Promotional

L.A. Gear (Footwear)

ILLUSTRATOR'S FORUM
ANNUAL EXHIBITION
OCTOBER 7 THROUGH 29 IN THE FOYER GALLERY OF NAZARETH COLLEGE
JOIN US FOR THE NINTH ANNUAL OPENING ON THURSDAY · OCTOBER 7 · 1993 · FROM 5:30 PM · GREAT FOOD · AMPLE DRINK AND ORIGINAL ART FROM ROCHESTER'S FINEST ILLUSTRATORS

Design and Illustration: Bob Conge

DESIGN FIRM:

Conge Design,

Rochester, New York

DESIGNER/ILLUSTRATOR:

Bob Conge

BUDGET: Pro bono

QUANTITY: 2500

PRINTING PROCESS:

4-color

PURPOSE: Exhibition

announcement

DESIGN FIRM:
Lambrenos Design,
Atco, New Jersey
ART DIRECTOR/
DESIGNER/ILLUSTRATOR:
Jim Lambrenos
PRINTER: Phototype
BUDGET: Pro bono
QUANTITY: 4000
PRINTING PROCESS:
4-color, process colors
added to black-and-white
art
PURPOSE: To designate
non-smoking areas.

ART DIRECTOR/

DESIGNER:

McRay Magleby/University

Publications, Provo, Utah

SILKSCREENER:

Rory Robinson

PURPOSE: Registration

reminder for students.

Brigham Young University

601 Design, Inc.

DESIGN FIRM:

601 Design, Inc.,

Denver, Colorado

ART DIRECTOR/

DESIGNER:

Bruce Holdeman

ILLUSTRATORS:

Bruce Holdeman,

JoRoan Lazaro

BUDGET: $975

QUANTITY: 500

PRINTING PROCESS:

4-color

PURPOSE: Studio poster/

promotional

*Below: 4-color separations
were reused from sublimated
bicycle jerseys for the Denver
Post "Ride the Rockies" bicycle
tour.*

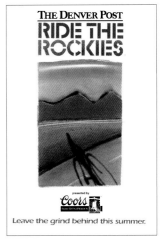

Choose from our daily selection of freshly baked bagels.

DISCOVER
The **better**
Bagel

DESIGN FIRM:

Runnion Design,

Lynnfield, Massachusetts

ART DIRECTOR/

DESIGNER: Jeff Runnion

PHOTOGRAPHER:

Jim Scherer

BUDGET: $11,000

QUANTITY: Produced in

two sizes—total 500

(double-sided) posters

PRINTING PROCESS:

4-color, offset

PURPOSE: To introduce

bagels.

Gold'n Plump. Preferred by chicken lovers everywhere.

AGENCY:

Clarity Coverdale Fury
Advertising, Inc.,
Minneapolis, Minnesota

ART DIRECTOR:

Randy Hughes

PHOTOGRAPHERS

Rick Dublin, Kerry Peterson

COPYWRITER: Bill Johnson